The Fifth French Republic

The Fifth French Republic

DOROTHY PICKLES

FREDERICK A. PRAEGER, *Publishers*

NEW YORK

BOOKS THAT MATTER

*Published in the United States of America
in 1960 by Frederick A. Praeger, Inc.,
Publishers, 64 University Place,
New York 3, N.Y.*

*Text © 1960 by Dorothy Pickles
Appendix © 1959 by William Pickles*

Library of Congress Catalog Card Number: 60-8738

THE FIFTH FRENCH REPUBLIC
is published in two editions:
  A Praeger Paperback (PPS-21)
  A clothbound edition

Printed in Great Britain

Contents

Preface

———————

The Constitution of 4th October 1958 does not merely break a great deal of new ground. It does so in ways that are exceedingly complex and difficult for the non-specialist to follow. Whatever may be said about its merits and demerits, it is certainly the most confused and obscure of France's many Constitutions since 1791. It is also, in a special sense, a *pièce de circonstance*. It was produced in the stress of a national emergency, when France had narrowly avoided a violent revolution, and under the inspiration of General de Gaulle who became the first President of the Fifth Republic. In the opinion of many of the critics of the new régime, it is unlikely to outlive his Presidency. But since it has already survived for more than a year and even on relatively pessimistic hypotheses may do so several more, it seemed justifiable and perhaps useful to try to describe what its purposes were and how far they are being achieved, even though it has been in existence for too short a time to make any final judgement possible.

The account is brief and has two main aims. They are, first, to try to place this Constitution in its political context and to make clear why and where it was a subject of controversy before it was voted; and second, to describe as simply as possible the institutions that it provides for, including the essential provisions of the numerous *Ordonnances* and organic laws which filled in some of the gaps during the six months following the promulgation of the Constitution itself. This second task has involved a certain amount of repetition, in the interests of clarity, owing to the complexity of the provisions

7

themselves. There are also, inevitably, a great many omissions. The present introductory study will need to be completed by much more detailed analysis and comment, as information becomes available on the actual working of the Constitution.

I should like to take this opportunity to thank M. Guy Mollet, M. and Mme Rosenfeld, M. Lucien Neuwirth, M. Léon Delbecque, M. Michel Massenet, M. Jacques Fauvet, M. Brilhac and Professor Gonidec of the University of Rennes for their kindness in answering questions, or supplying information on a number of points.

November 1959   DOROTHY PICKLES

CHAPTER I

The Republican Tradition

Constitutional experiments

No study of the French Constitution can make its intentions plain
unless it takes account of the factor of heredity. For in the field of
constitution-making the French hold a world record. It has often
been said that, since 1789, France has changed her Constitution on
an average every 12 years. Such a statement needs amplification,
for the average covers extremes in time ranging from the 21 days of
the *acte additionnel* of 1815 to the 65 years of the Third Republic,
and extremes in content ranging from complete changes of régime
to modifications no greater than some carried out by the normal
processes of constitutional revision. Moreover, it is difficult to find
an agreed definition on which to base the calculation. Should only
written Constitutions be counted, although some (those of 1793
and 1814) were not applied? Or, if only those Constitutions are
counted which were actually put into force, should provisional
régimes be included which were based on no written text (those of
1792–5, 1848, 1871–5, 1940–4 and 1944–6)?

The three cycles

Perhaps a more useful way of looking at French constitutional experiments is to concentrate attention less on how often they happened,
and on the specific changes that each introduced, than on the general
picture of constitutional evolution over the 170 years since the
French revolution. During this period, movement from one system

to another seems to form a pattern, repeated in three distinct cycles.[1] It is essential not to distort the facts in order to make this pattern tidier or more consistent than it really is. But though the parallel is not complete the general resemblances are marked. Constitutional Monarchy gives way to Republic and the Republic in turn is replaced by some form of dictatorial government. The first cycle may be said to begin with the Constitution of 1791 which was that of a Constitutional Monarchy. In 1792, the Monarchy gave way to Republican government and France was at war by the time the first Republican Constitution had been voted in 1793. It was never applied and indeed, it has been argued that it was inapplicable. That of 1795 already reflected the reaction against the revolutionary Governments of the Convention. Its main aim was to protect France from popular rule of this kind and it, therefore, incorporated a number of checks and balances which made it, in practice, unworkable. There followed in rapid succession the Constitutions of the years VIII, X, and XII which reflected the rise to power of Napoleon, who became Emperor in 1804.

The second cycle may be said to begin with the return of Louis XVIII, after the defeat of Napoleon in 1815.[2] It presents some variants but the general course of evolution is similar. The monarchy, for instance, underwent a double evolution, becoming first less liberal under Charles X, and then more parliamentary under the July monarchy. The change was political rather than constitutional, the text of the Charter of 1830 presenting few differences from that of 1814. The Second Republic, whose constitution lasted only three years, was followed by the coup d'état of 1851 and the Second

[1] v. Les Constitutions de la France by Maurice Duverger (Presses Universitaires de France, 1944) which develops this idea in considerable detail. M. Duverger, however, does not regard the period from 1875 onwards as constituting a third cycle.

[2] The choice of this date involves considerable oversimplification. It ignores the Senatorial Constitution of 1814, monarchical in all but name, which was never applied, and the Imperial acte additionnel which was; and it takes no account of the resemblances between the Senatorial Constitution and the Charter of the same year.

Empire, which lasted from 1852 to France's defeat in the War of
1870. It was twice liberalized, the second time only a few weeks
before the Empire collapsed.

The third cycle, beginning with the voting of the constitution
of the Third Republic in 1875, presents some special features.
First, it does not begin with Monarchy. But the second liberali-
zation of the Imperial Constitution transformed it into something like a constitutional monarchy, and the 1875 Constitution
is often described as one of *attente monarchique*. It was, in fact,
drawn up by an Assembly which included a majority of Mon-
archists, and in such a way as to facilitate a transition from Republic to Monarchy—a transition which was never made. In
other words, the period opens with a would-be monarchic phase,
followed by over 60 years of Republican government. The Vichy
régime which followed it in 1940 was provisional, and the German
occupation of half the country up to 1942 and the whole country
from 1942 onwards meant that Governments were largely dependent
on the goodwill of the occupier. It would, in all probability have been
impossible to hold any elections. Nevertheless, the régime was
dictatorial in the sense that its general principles reflected the known
anti-democratic opinions of prominent sections of French society
(though not exclusively—the collaborators also included progressive elements) and in that it was regarded by many French Republicans as being *la revanche de 1936*.

Though no Constitution was ever promulgated, a number of
so-called 'Constitutional Acts' (in reality executive decisions)
were put into force and there were administrative changes, the whole
constituting what was described as 'the National Revolution',
whose motto was *Travail, famille, patrie* and whose aim was the
creation of a kind of nineteenth-century paternalist and corporatist
dictatorship.

It ended, not with defeat, but with the allied victory of 1944–5.
But the circumstances of that victory as they concerned France produced some of the reflexes of defeat. France was less a liberating
than a liberated country; her armed forces played only a minor, if

vital, rôle. Up to 1946, France felt that the other three great Power were treating her as a poor relation. She suffered, therefore, fo some years following the war from an over-sensitivity that ofte looked very like the kind of inferiority complex produced by defeat This affected the politics of the Fourth Republic and so affected th fortunes of the Constitution of 1946.

Is France entering a fourth cycle?

If the Fourth Republic represents, as it certainly does in the mind of some Frenchmen, the beginning of a fourth cycle, the earl stages are dissimilar from those of the first three, and the end o the cycle is still in the future. The first difference is that it has n monarchical or even would-be monarchical initial phase. On th contrary, the provisional Government, headed by General d Gaulle, set out in 1945 to draw up a Republican Constitution tha would express the permanent victory of Republican and democrati Parliamentary government.

For what emerges from the preceding brief summary of France' constitutional experiments since 1789, even if the suggested cyclica pattern is rejected as an oversimplification or as a somewhat fancifu distortion of the facts, is that no régime has up to now succeeded i establishing itself firmly enough to feel immune from the danger o attempts to overthrow it. Even the three-quarters of a century o the Third Republic—the longest-lived of any régime since 1789— has been described as:

> an epoch in which the idea of democracy never quite secures it letters of credit and the idea of reaction never quite dares openly to organize itself as a party seeking to overthrow democrati foundations.[1]

In 1940, with the aid of a war, the democratic foundations had been overthrown once again, but the two Constituent Assemblie

[1] H. J. Laski, in the preface to *France is a Democracy*, Louis Lévy (Gollancz, 1943), p. 9.

of 1945–6 were overwhelmingly Republican and democratic in outlook. Even if the Communists are left out of account, the 544 Deputies who sat for metropolitan France included over 300 representatives of democratic and predominantly left-wing parties. They hoped to remove, at long last, from the field of political controversy the question of what political system was best suited to France, and to produce that degree of unanimity regarding the political machinery that Lord Balfour has described as essential to the effective working of parliamentary government.

It soon became apparent that this aim was not to be achieved. For by 1951 almost one elector in two was voting for a candidate representing a party (either Gaullist or Communist) that rejected the parliamentary system, at least in the form it took under the Fourth Republic. By 1953–5, right-wing extremist movements had made their appearance, some of which resembled the kind of anti-Republican and anti-Parliamentary challenge that had characterized the last decade of the Third Republic, though one only—the Poujadist movement—could claim to have made any serious impact on opinion.

When the challenge did come, however, in 1958, it presented quite a number of unique features. The revolution that led to the collapse of the Fourth Republic broke out, not in Paris, but in Algiers. The immediate cause was less the situation in France than the impact of events in France on the future of Algeria, and the immediate threat to France came in the main from certain sections of the army, in particular from those who were serving, or had served, in parachute regiments in Algeria. The end of the régime came without bloodshed and by technically legal and constitutional processes. It could not with accuracy be described as a victory for the revolutionaries, since the new Government included most of the Ministers who had held office in the previous one, and was supported by a majority of all parties except the Communist Party. The new Constitution was intended by the majority of those who drew it up to be both Republican and democratic and was accepted by an overwhelming majority of the population in the referendum of the 28th September 1958.

Some opponents of the new régime argued that, whatever the intentions of those who drew it up, the constitution would prove unworkable, at latest, when General de Gaulle was no longer head of the State. For them, the new régime constituted a move away from the Republican tradition, the first stage of the journey along a familiar road. They saw 1959 as equivalent to 1798 or 1851, both of which were preludes to dictatorship. Others, again, argued that, whatever the merits or demerits of the Constitution, the future of the Republic depended on General de Gaulle who was now 'the sole remaining rampart between the Republic and Fascism'.[1]

These divisions of opinions are explicable only in two essential contexts. The first is that of the French Republican tradition, as it has evolved during these numerous constitutional changes. The second is that of the events which constituted the immediate prelude to the Fifth Republic.

The Republican tradition

It is not easy to describe with any degree of completeness or precision what really constitutes the Republican tradition, because it is not a series of dogmas but rather a number of beliefs and emotions about the kind of relationship that ought to exist between State and citizen and between Government and legislature. These beliefs and emotions go very deep because Frenchmen have had to fight and die for them so often in their history, because memories of the most recent eclipse of democracy and Republicanism are still vivid, at least in the minds of all Frenchmen over thirty, and because some Frenchmen are still far from convinced that they will not have to fight for them again in the near future.

But exactly what they have fought for, or will fight for, is something that defies exact analysis, primarily for two reasons. First, not all Republicans are agreed on the meaning to be attached to the term; and second, the language in which the feelings are expressed has become a kind of political shorthand, summing up episodes of

[1] Jacques Fauvet in *Le Monde*, 29–30.6.58.

rench history and attitudes to significant events or conflicts. Some
f the language has by now become symbolic. It is difficult to sort
ut the relative importance of history and politics in phrases and
vords like 'The Republic, one and indivisible', 'the sacred right of
nsurrection', 'the rights of man and the citizen', 'popular sov-
reignty', 'equal and secret ballots', 'a secular, democratic, and social
Republic'. They are now symbols of a *mystique*. They form part of
ne picture that some Frenchmen have of the Republic. General
e Gaulle began his memoirs as follows:

> All my life, France has had a quite special meaning for me,
> that is based on sentiment as much as on reason.

very Frenchman's Republic has a quite special meaning for him,
oo. But it is not always the same Republic.

In the minds of most Socialists, and of some Radicals, the Revolu-
ionary tradition—the belief that modern France dates from 1789—
s an integral part of the Republican tradition. André Siegfried
lescribed this attitude in the '30's:

> A century and a half after the declaration of the rights of man,
> the French Revolution is still something on which there is no
> unanimity. The differences have nothing to do with a Repub-
> lican or a Monarchic régime; they go much deeper. Leon Bour-
> geois understood this perfectly when, after the Boulangist
> affair, he replied to a number of Royalists prepared for a *rap-
> prochement* with the régime: 'It is not merely a matter of accepting
> the Republic. Do you accept the Revolution?'[1]

Some of the constitution-makers of 1946 were very conscious of
his Revolutionary inheritance. M. Mollet, for instance, when
e became President of the Constitutional Commission in March
946, stated that it intended to remain faithful to the Declaration of
789 and had it constantly in mind, 'as it has the texts of 1793, of
arious allied countries and that drawn up in 1936 by the League

[1] *Tableau des Partis en France* (Paris, Grasset, 1930), p. 57.

of the Rights of Man'. In the Socialist calendar, Whit Sunday when martyrs of the *Commune* are remembered at the *Mur de Fédérés*, is as important as the 14th of July, for, in the minds of French Socialists, Socialism and Republicanism are inseparable.

Radicals, whose ideal of political equality is also inspired by 1789, by no means always subscribe to all the social implications that appear to Socialists as the natural twentieth-century expression of the principle of equality. Radical Republicanism has tended to emphasize spiritual and intellectual equality, to support anti-clericalism and educational opportunity—*la carrière ouverte aux talents*—and to allow economic equality often to take a back seat. More right-wing politicians, such as Doumergue, Poincaré, or M. Coty, all of whom were Presidents of the Republic whose authentic Republicanism was never in question, were less concerned with general principles and more with techniques of government, and, in particular, with the need for strong government. In general, right-wing Republicans have tended to associate left-wing revolutionary Republicanism with a liking for weak governments.

In spite of these and other divergences, it is possible to single out at least three tendencies that are essentially characteristic of the French Republican tradition. The first is the insistence on the importance of the individual citizen and on his right to certain freedoms regarded as fundamental. In institutional terms this has shown itself in a predilection for complex electoral systems designed to reflect (though not always with mathematical accuracy) as large a gamut as possible of political opinions and in the inclusion in Constitutions of tributes to a certain number of these freedoms. The use of the word 'tributes' is deliberate. For since the rights, or freedoms in question are not easily guaranteed either by Constitutions or Courts of law, some of them remain in the realm of hope, or theory, rather than of fact. The Constitutions of 1791, 1793, 1795, 1848, 1946 and 1958 all included Declarations of Rights, either directly or by reference.[1]

---

[1] They usually reaffirm the rights contained in the 1789 Declaration of the Rights of Man, which was incorporated in the 1791 Constitution, though the

The second tendency is one that seeks to exalt the popularly elected Assembly at the expense of both the Second Chamber and the Government. In its most left-wing, or Revolutionary, expression it is a belief in Conventional government, or *gouvernement d'assemblée*; in its most right-wing expression it becomes little more than a defence of the prestige of Parliament and of the right of Deputies to play a more independent rôle and to take a greater share in legislative initiative, and in legislative processes generally, than would be acceptable to either Government or Opposition parties in the British Parliament. Both right and left-wing Republicans hold that the essential rôle and the unchallengeable right of Parliament is to vote the laws and to decide what are suitable subjects for legislation. Within this framework, the function of the Government is to execute the laws. In the words of article 6 of the Declaration of the Rights of Man:

> The laws are the expression of the general will. All citizens have the right to participate in legislation, either directly or through their representatives.

Gouvernement d'assemblée, the encroachment by Parliament on what might legitimately be considered to be the executive sphere, has been responsible, more than any other single factor, for the weakness and incoherence of French Governments and so has led to reactions against it, some of which have rejected the Parliamentary system along with its weaknesses. But although there is always a danger that a movement for strong government may develop into a challenge to the régime, and always a fear in the minds

1795 Constitution shows a marked lack of enthusiasm for rights and a strong consciousness of duties. The 1946 and 1958 Constitutions go farther than the 1789 Declaration, the former adding a number of social and economic rights, such as the right to strike, to employment, to join the trade union of one's choice, to social security and educational opportunity, the latter subscribing in general to all of these, without special mention of any. The Consultative Constitutional Committee had proposed in 1958 to subscribe also to the rights mentioned in the Universal Declaration of Human Rights of 1948, but the Government rejected this amendment.

B

of some Frenchmen that such movements will do so, because it has happened in the past, it is important to emphasize that the distinction between what have been called, for convenience, the left-wing and right-wing Republican traditions is by no means clear or consistent. Some left-wing Prime Ministers of the Fourth Republic, in particular, M. Mollet and M. Pflimlin, were in favour of amending the constitution of the Fourth Republic in order to strengthen Governments. M. Pflimlin succeeded in getting some of these amendments voted on the day preceding his resignation, and these two Ministers are popularly credited with the responsibility for the inclusion in the 1958 Constitution of provisions remarkably similar to two of them.[1] On the other hand, though the supporters of a Presidential, or quasi-Presidential, system have been in the main on the right, it has also found eminent supporters on the left, even if only temporarily.[2] When the 1958 Constitution was in preparation, and in 1959, when the Standing Orders of both Assemblies were under discussion, some right-wing Deputies and Senators showed themselves to be no less fervent defenders of the rights of Parliament than their colleagues on the left.

What tends to separate Right and Left is often less the content of specific measures than the undertones for which history is responsible. The Left, for instance, remembers that the Directoire was followed by Napoleon, the second Republic by Louis Napoleon and the Third by Pétain, and is afraid of history repeating itself; the Right is conscious of the overlapping of Republican and Revolutionary traditions on the Left; of the fact that the first Republic developed into the Convention and the Terror, that Socialism was associated with the Second Republic and that the Third was heralded by the Commune, and so is equally afraid of history repeating itself in a different way. It can also, for instance, be

---

[1] Articles 41 and 49; v. infra, pp. 103–10, 114–18.

[2] Léon Blum wrote in favour of a Presidential system for France in 1946, but very shortly changed his mind. In 1956 there were a number of discussions of this question by politicians and political scientists, some on the left being attracted by it.

generally assumed that on a certain number of issues, in particular those involving the rights of Catholic schools and of Parliament, the desirability of State control of the economy and a generous system of social security, or of the merits of this or that electoral system, a majority of each tendency will be found in opposite camps.

Whether this pull between right- and left-wing Republicanism remains within the régime or not depends on a number of factors; on their relative strengths, on the extent to which each side can achieve some internal unity, instead of being split by issues like anti-clericalism, or nationalization, which today cut across the traditional divisions between Republicans more than in the past, and it also depends on external circumstances. External danger has always made it easier for right-wing Republicanism to slide into acquiescence in extremism. The defeat of both the First and the Third Republics was assisted, if not brought about, by war. In 1958 war also played a part in bringing the Fourth Republic to an end, though it was a rebellion in Algeria and not a foreign war. It also depends on the way in which Republican Constitutions are applied. And this is a factor which explains some of the uncertainty in the minds of many Frenchmen regarding the future evolution of the Fifth Republic.

The oscillations characteristic of French constitutional and political history over the past 170 years have in themselves contributed to the growth of a third Republican tradition which might be more accurately described as a constitutional attitude, characteristic of Republicans and anti-Republicans alike. It is an attitude of political rigidity, or intolerance, which is caused by the sense of constitutional instability. The fact that no régime is sure of its capacity to survive leads each in turn to look to its defences from the start, to seek to strengthen the régime by turning the Constitution into a strait-jacket for potential wreckers. It does so by concentrating attention on known and familiar dangers and by trying to make hard and fast rules to deal with them.[1] In practice, this has

---

[1] Cf. M. Duverger, *Les Institutions de la Cinquième République*, in *Revue française de Science Politique*, March, 1959, p. 101. 'Every Constitution is a political weapon, used by a victorious party in order to consolidate its victory.'

often turned out to be a design for winning the last war. For each régime brings its own problems, which are often quite different from those of its predecessor. It was often said, for instance, that those who drew up the 1946 Constitution were haunted by de Gaulle and by the ghosts of the two Napoleons, Boulanger and Pétain. But the strait-jacket designed for them proved ineffective against the real challenge, which came from a quarter that had not been foreseen in 1946. The 1946 Constitution provided a complex procedure designed to prevent the deadlock between the Senate and the directly elected Assembly that had been one of the acknowledged weaknesses of the Third Republic. In case of conflict the Assembly's will was to prevail. But, in practice, this will was itself often para-lysed by divisions which the constitutional machinery could do nothing to eliminate. The Constitution of 1946 was, in theory, flexible and the amending process simple. In practice, it took four years to achieve some minor, mainly technical, reforms and there followed three years of deadlock during which agreement was not even reached regarding the amendment of the amending process itself. It is perhaps no coincidence that the longest-lived of France's Republican Constitutions was the shortest and most flexible, not because its authors were more confident of the régime's capacity to survive but, on the contrary, because they were trying in ad-vance to leave elbow room for the Monarchy that they hoped would replace it.

It is not only that Constitutions cannot guarantee to safeguard the future. There are also some ills for which Constitutions have no cure and among them are deep and bitter political divisions. For most of the life of the Fourth Republic a large number of both its electors and its Parliamentary representatives on the Right and on the Left were bitterly opposed both to each other and to the régime. The Communists, it is true, did not in theory object to the Constitu-tion, but in practice they prevented it from working properly. And even the parties that were attached to the régime were often so divided that the Assembly and Governments were alike powerless to act. Among the problems that gave rise to these divisions, the inadequacies of the Constitution were probably the least important. If Parliaments had known where they wanted to go, they might well have been able to agree on the reforms needed to make the Constitution a more efficient instrument for getting them there. As it was, the problem of constitutional reform, which ought to have been merely a minor irritant, became a major time-waster and added one more to the list of unsolved and insoluble problems that finally killed the régime.

This is not, of course, the view of General de Gaulle. He had opposed the Constitution from the start, resigned from the premiership and retired from politics before it came into force. It was only natural that on his return to power 12 years later he should have refused to accept institutions that he had always considered deplorable. Besides, by that time, many Frenchmen, too, had come to treat the Constitution as the scapegoat for the failings of the Fourth Republic.

This is not to say that the majority of Frenchmen thought that the kind of Constitution that General de Gaulle had in mind would be an improvement. In the prolonged debate on constitutional reform that took place in Parliament and press from 1955 onwards, the proposed remedies had followed, in the main, more conventional lines. Comment on the provisions of the new Constitution from August to the referendum on the 28th September 1958 was largely hostile, only the Gaullists being wholeheartedly approving. Yet 79·25 per cent of the voters in metropolitan France, and an even higher proportion in Algeria and the Overseas Territories, voted YES. It is essential, therefore, to consider briefly the events which led to the end of the Fourth Republic and which persuaded so many Frenchmen to accept without question a Constitution whose most criticized provisions were out of harmony, if not in conflict, with the Republican traditions as expressed in the Constitutions of earlier Republics.

CHAPTER II

Prelude to the Fifth Republic

Though a crisis of the régime had been predicted for a long time, the event that finally sparked off the explosion in May 1958 did not at first appear to present an immediate danger to the régime. A demonstration by the European population of Algiers, intended to prevent the Government then in process of formation in Paris from contemplating any form of negotiation with the Algerian nationalists, was nothing new. There had been demonstrations with similar aims on 6th February 1956, when M. Mollet visited Algeria, and in March and April 1958. Nor could a riot, or even a revolution, in Algeria, have constituted by itself a threat to France. Algerians were dependent on the French army to protect them from terrorist attacks and the army was, in turn, dependent on France for its supplies. It was generally estimated that Algeria could have been starved into submission within a fortnight.

The importance of public opinion

At least four circumstances combined to turn the demonstration into a fortnight-long campaign for a Government headed by General de Gaulle—a campaign which ended in victory. The first was the absence on the part of public and politicians alike of any real will to defend the Fourth Republic. Disillusionment and cynicism had been growing since 1949, largely owing to persistent deadlock in the

Assembly and to the consequent instability of Governments and their inability to take urgent and necessary decisions. Deadlock over the Indo-Chinese war and over E.D.C. had been followed by deadlock over Tunisia and Morocco. From 1955 onwards, there had been deadlock over both constitutional and electoral reform and over the future of Algeria, where a nationalist rebellion had broken out in the Aurès mountains at the end of 1954. By 1958, the rebellion showed no signs of being overcome, though it was by then costing between £1 and £2 million a day, holding down the bulk of the French army in Algeria, creating problems for France in N.A.T.O., in the United Nations and in her relations with Morocco and Tunisia. Between May 1957 and April 1958, three Governments had fallen, directly or indirectly owing to North African problems, and primarily to the Algerian rebellion. The effect of all these deadlocks was to create a growing disrespect on the part of the public for Parliament and for politicians.

The predominant atmosphere in France was one of political apathy. In the ranks of the army and the higher Civil Service there was some positive opposition. The Minister of the Interior in M. Pflimlin's Government, M. Jules Moch, revealed later that, when faced on the 13th May with an insurrection in Algiers, followed by an insurrection in Corsica, planned and carried out by participants in the Algiers movement, the Government had discovered that it could no longer rely on the loyalty of a number of army leaders, of the police, and of civilian officials. Some of these rebellious elements were Gaullist, others were not. There were also some Gaullists among French Deputies, though it is generally admitted that, when the insurrection began, there was not sufficient active support in the French Parliament to enable General de Gaulle to be voted into power constitutionally. The majority of the civilian population, both inside and outside Parliament, was certainly neither Gaullist nor anti-Republican. But neither politicians nor public showed any sign of readiness to die on the barricades for the French Republic. M. Mollet is said to have remarked during the crisis:

> There is talk of firing our last shots, but we have not yet fired our first.[1]

Those first shots never were fired.

There are a number of possible explanations of this state of affairs: economic prosperity had helped to increase political apathy; even if large sections of the army had been loyal to the régime, to add a war in France to the existing war in Algeria would have been militarily risky and psychologically difficult; there was no real political leadership, no faith in the success of resistance and no agreement on how to set about it; the facts of the situation were confused and most people (including members of Parliament) had little real knowledge of what was happening. All this adds up to one conclusion. There may be doubts regarding the real strength of the movement that threatened France with a *coup d'état*. There can be none regarding the real weakness of the Republican will to resist. As more than one commentator pointed out, the Republic was not murdered; it committed suicide.[2]

The importance of the 13th May

The circumstance which helped to make General de Gaulle's return possible was the transformation of the Algiers demonstration into a movement in which settlers and army leaders in Algeria combined to demand a Government of Public Safety, headed by General de Gaulle—a movement which, as time went on, won growing support in France.

This was the work of the different 'plotters'—'Colonels' or civilians—about whom so much has since been written. Whether there were, in reality, '13 plots of the 13th May' is unimportant. There were certainly three distinct attitudes, which had to be focused on General de Gaulle if the insurrection were to succeed.

[1] Quoted on p. 312 of *Les 13 Complots du 13 Mai*, by Merry and Serge Bromberger. (Paris, Arthème Fayard, 1959.)

[2] *v.* for instance, Sirius, *le Suicide de la IVe République* (Editions du Cerf, 1958) and Jean Ferniot, *les Ides de Mai* (Plon, 1958), p. 1, 'The Fourth Republic . . . died alone, with no friends at the bedside.'

The interest of the extreme right-wing settlers—the 'ultras' was concentrated on Algeria, on the need for Algeria to remain French. They were determined to prevent Algeria from going the way of Morocco and Tunisia and becoming an independent State. The European minority would then have to choose between leaving the country, which was impossible for the majority, made up of small tradesmen or officials, and becoming citizens of a backward Moslem country. The settlers were not Gaullist and had not even been Gaullist during the war, when General de Gaulle's provisional Government had its headquarters in Algiers.

The aims of the army—or more accurately of those of its leaders and officers who were opposed to the policies of Governments of the Fourth Republic, a small number of whom were also involved in more or less subversive organizations—were much more complex. They shared the opposition of the 'ultras' to negotiation with the Moslem nationalists, though for different reasons. After so many humiliations in Indo-China, Morocco and Tunisia, army leaders wanted a victory. Many of the junior officers who had been responsible for the protection of the Moslem population from terrorist attacks had also come to the conclusion that military victory alone would not be enough to keep Algeria permanently bound to France. They believed in an extensive programme of economic and social reform in order to raise the standard of living of the Moslems and to make them 'first-class' Frenchmen (*des Français à part entière*). This was the policy known as 'integration'.[1] Although the settler population had for years resisted strenuously attempts to give the Moslem population something nearer to real equality, they accepted this programme, in May 1958, partly as the necessary price of army

[1] The objective of integration has been defined as: 'the indissoluble union of former colonial peoples and the former mother country within a single political entity, with the aim of establishing equality of rights and duties, and, in the long run, an equalization of the standard of living'. (P. F. Gonidec, *Droit d'Outre-Mer*, Paris, Editions Montchrestien, 1959, p. 331.) If the real aims of the 'ultras' were to be judged by their actions over the previous ten years, it was evident that where the equalization of the standard of living was concerned, 'the long term' was likely to be very long indeed.

support, without which the insurrection must necessarily fail, and partly because they would fear equality less in an Algeria administered as if it were part of metropolitan France. It is also true, as became evident later, that, for some of the settler organizations, the acceptance of 'integration' was a temporary expedient, and that, once their primary aim of *l'Algérie française* had become accepted French policy, the implications of 'integration' could be reconsidered.

Some of the army leaders, who, as part of their task of protecting the Moslem population, had been carrying out a whole series of administrative functions, had come to the conclusion that the best solution for Algeria would be for the army to rule. They were contemptuous of the quarrels of French Parliaments and the vacillations of French Governments, which, as they saw it, had already cost France most of her former Empire and were now threatening the loss of Algeria. They resented being called on to fight a war in conditions which seemed to them to prevent a military victory and, at the same time, to undermine the army's efforts to win over the civilian population. In particular, they rejected even the suggestion of possible negotiations with the rebels, partly because of their determination not to be cheated of a military victory, but partly because they regarded negotiations as a betrayal of the loyal Moslem population. This last opinion was especially strong among young Captains in the S.A.S. (*Sections administratives spéciales*) who had been working and living with Moslems in the villages, acting as teachers, doctors, magistrates, engineers and administrators. Their argument was a simple one. Negotiations meant victory for the rebels. That would mean torture and death for Moslems who had been co-operating with the French and who had relied on the French army to protect them. It could not be expected, therefore, that Moslems would continue to trust the French, if there were to be talk of negotiations. The war was psychologically lost in advance if the French were not determined to win it. And if civilian Governments were not capable of this determination, then it was for the army to replace them.

This view was not characteristic of the army as a whole. Indeed, there is no such entity as 'the army'. In a country such as France, in which military service is traditional, the army is a cross section of the nation. It is also a service apart from the nation, since many of its regular officers have been engaged overseas ever since the end of the war, and it was among the regular *cadres* that most of the subversive elements were to be found. But there was no unanimity. The army, too, has its Republican traditions, among which that of *la grande muette*—the view that the army's function is to leave politics to the civilians—is still strong. Probably only a small minority wanted power for the army; the rest wanted power, instead of weakness, to be the attribute of the French State. Some held that only a Government headed by General de Gaulle could guarantee this.

Both army and 'ultras', then, were agreed that French victory in Algeria was essential and that French Governments were too weak and divided to guarantee it. They were not agreed on the kind of Government that *was* needed in France, nor on the methods by which a change of Government could be achieved.

The third element in the revolution of 13th May was made up of what are generally called 'Gaullists'. They were in agreement with the two objectives of military victory and the retention of Algeria as part of France and, in addition, convinced that only a French Government headed by General de Gaulle could be relied on to achieve them. Some believed also in 'integration'; others believed it to be a totally unrealistic and Utopian dream, both psychologically and economically impossible, but constituting, nevertheless, an invaluable instrument of propaganda, capable of rallying European and Moslem Algerians, together with the army, to support for General de Gaulle. They proved to be right—or, perhaps more accurately, the efforts of a number of able politicians were successful in turning it into such an instrument.

The important point is that this third element regarded Algeria as a means rather than an end. The aim of the Gaullist conspirators—for there was a conspiracy, indeed several, involving a number of

Gaullist politicians and army officers—was to change the system of Government in France. But beyond the aim of getting rid of the Fourth Republic and securing General de Gaulle's return to power, there was no unity between different personalities and movements. Some supporters of the revolution of 13th May were frankly Fascists, in the tradition of the early '30's; some were nearer to the reactionary conservatism of the Algerian 'ultras' or of M. Poujade; some were, or claimed to be, socially progressive; some were pinning their faith to new institutions, others to the leadership of General de Gaulle; some were concentrating on methods, on the first step, which was the success of the Revolution, and leaving the rest for later consideration; some were conspirators, active plotters, others disillusioned Republicans or former resisters with a nostalgic hangover from the years of underground fighting; some were idealistic Gaullists, others hard-headed politicians.

During the fortnight from 13th May to 1st June, these different currents of opinion were concentrated on achieving two things: a Government in Paris, headed by General de Gaulle (it being assumed by those who were determined that Algeria should remain French that General de Gaulle shared their views); and the acceptance by such a Government of the policy of 'integration', in order to win over Moslem opinion to France. This result was achieved partly thanks to preparatory work carried out for some months by French politicians in Algeria, in particular by M. Delbecque, then a member of the *cabinet* of the Minister of Defence, M. Chaban Delmas, who was himself a Gaullist; partly thanks to spectacular demonstrations of 'Franco-Moslem fraternization', which convinced a number of sceptics regarding the possibility of *l'Algérie française* that 'integration' might after all be a practical policy; partly by threats of an imminent military *coup d'état* in France and by an actual landing in Corsica, both of which convinced many people of the reality of disaffection in the army and the Civil Service; and partly by the oratorical gifts of M. Soustelle, a Gaullist Deputy and a former Governor-General of Algeria, extremely popular with the Algiers population, who landed in Algiers on 17th May, having evaded a police guard on his house in Paris.

The degree of unity between all these different tendencies, whether in France or in Algeria, was limited to the two objectives already mentioned. Each had its own conception of what General de Gaulle would, or ought to, do. None knew for certain the conditions on which he would agree even to assume power.

The importance of General de Gaulle

General de Gaulle emerged from his retirement to make three public statements during the crisis. The first, on 15th May, expressed his readiness 'to assume the powers of the Republic'; the second, on 19th May, was a press conference at which he stated that he would do so only by legal means; the third, on 27th May, stated that he had 'set in motion the regular procedure necessary for the establishment of a Republican Government capable of ensuring the unity and independence of the country'.

The effect of these statements was to encourage support for him both in the army and in the French Parliament. The former felt that he agreed with the army's point of view (he had explicitly praised the army's work in Algeria at the press conference, while making no reference to the landing in Corsica, which was, of course, a *coup d'état*) and that victory was at hand. Parliamentarians were reassured regarding his intention to respect Republican legality. On the issue that above all divided the country nothing was said at all, which enabled Frenchmen, from Socialists to extreme Right, to come to quite contradictory conclusions regarding his policy for Algeria. General de Gaulle was really given a blank cheque on Algeria, though not everybody intended to do so, for, once he had come to power, those who found that their assumptions were incorrect had to put up with the situation. Revolutions cannot be made every month.

The importance of Parliament

The last obstacle, the investiture of General de Gaulle as Prime Minister, was the most formidable. Three things helped to overcome it: a message to both Houses of Parliament by the President of the Republic, threatening to resign if General de Gaulle's candidature to the Premiership was not accepted; concessions by Parliament; and concessions by General de Gaulle.

General de Gaulle's readiness to 'assume the powers of the Republic' was conditional on the grant of special powers to govern by decree for six months, during which period his Government was to draw up a new Constitution to be approved by a referendum. Parliament was to go into recess (the session could not constitutionally be closed as it had not lasted for the seven months required by Article 9). Parliament was, of course, free to accept or reject both his investiture and these conditions. The difficulty, from General de Gaulle's point of view, was to prevent Deputies from debating and seeking to amend them, as he had no intention of becoming involved in the political bargaining normally characteristic of both investiture and legislation. On the other hand, investiture by the National Assembly, the revision of Article 90 of the Constitution, governing the amending process (the procedure that had been envisaged by General de Gaulle was not in accordance with that laid down in the Constitution), and the passage of a law granting the special powers, were the only legal and constitutional ways by which his conditions could be met.

What happened was that, after a brief declaration by General de Gaulle, the investiture debate took place in his absence, though he was present during the debate on the Bill to revise Article 90 of the Constitution. Parliament agreed to vote the Bill without amendment, and General de Gaulle's Government undertook, in drawing up the Constitution, to respect five basic conditions: to retain the principle of universal suffrage, the responsibility of the Government to Parliament, the separation of legislative and executive power, the independence of the judiciary, and to provide for the possibility of 'organizing the relations between the Republic and the associated peoples'. General de Gaulle also gave further reassurances to the Assembly in person, in particular that, in the new Constitution, the offices of President and Prime Minister would remain distinct.

All the same, the investiture vote was not obtained easily. Nor do these concessions in themselves explain why so many Deputies on the non-Communist Left voted for General de Gaulle on 1st June and why they advised their supporters to vote for the Constitution on 28th September. Most parties except the Communists were divided and the Socialist Parliamentary Group debated for a whole day before deciding, by 77 votes to 74,[1] to support General de Gaulle's investiture. Even this narrow margin was achieved only after a visit to Colombey-les-deux-Eglises by M. Mollet, M. Auriol and the leader of the Socialist group in the Assembly, M. Deixonne. The Mendésiste section of the Radicals and the U.D.S.R. leader, M. Mitterand remained opposed, as did, of course, the Communist party. In the end, though 329 Deputies voted for General de Gaulle, 229 voted against, including 49 of the 96 Socialist Deputies.

The decision of the majority of the non-Communist Left (Socialists, Radicals and M.R.P.) to vote for the new Constitution was really governed by three factors, none of which was really relevant to the merits, or demerits, of the Constitution. The first was the fear of a military dictatorship. This argument was put forcibly during the referendum campaign by a number of leaders, from M. Reynaud on the Right to M. Mollet on the Left. The choice was: ' de Gaulle ou les paras '. For some this fear was twofold. It was that a military dictatorship would be merely a first stage, leading to a Popular Front. Those who opposed this argument, in particular M. Mendès-France, objected to a vote which they held to be 'under duress'. M. Mendès-France argued later[2] that General de Gaulle,

---

[1] These figures include the Socialist Senators. Of the Deputies, 51 voted against and only 44 for.

[2] v. for instance, his lecture at Chatham House on 25 February 1959, reported in *International Affairs*, July 1959.

instead of constituting a protection against a military dictatorship
was in danger of becoming, against his will, the prisoner of those
forces who want one. The weakness of the opposition was that it
was small, divided, leaderless and without any concerted policy or
plan of campaign.

The second factor was the conviction in the minds of many
Frenchmen that General de Gaulle alone in France had sufficient
prestige to be able to achieve some solution of the Algerian problem
and to restore the authority of the State over the dissident elements
in the army and the public service. Some trusted him to find a
solution, whatever it might be; others to find a progressive solution,
others to win the war and maintain *l'Algérie française*.

The third factor was the conviction that General de Gaulle had
progressive views regarding the evolution of the Overseas Territories. This opinion was, perhaps, more than anything else responsible for the decision of the majority of the Socialist party to support the Constitution. It was indubitably decisive in the territories
themselves. In July, a number of political leaders in the Overseas
Territories had openly expressed their disappointment that the first
draft of the Constitution had included no recognition of their right
to independence. A Congress of the *Parti du Regroupement Africain*
had passed a resolution in favour of immediate independence.
General de Gaulle's promise that France would not prevent any
Territory from seceding, and the provision in the definitive text of
possibilities of evolution, not excluding independence, decided the
leaders of all but one Territory to vote in favour of the Constitution.

In all these arguments, the actual content of the Constitution
was, more often than not, left out of account altogether. This is not
to say that there was no discussion of the Constitution itself. On
the contrary, press and periodicals in France were full of comment;
political parties discussed its weaknesses; political scientists analysed
it. In general, as has been said, opinion was unfavourable, with the
exception, naturally, of Gaullist opinion. But there is no doubt that
the referendum of the 28th September 1958 was not, in reality, a

vote for a Constitution, but a vote for General de Gaulle. The Constitution was, for most of those who thought about it at all, merely part of the price that had to be paid for his continued presence at the head of affairs.

All these happenings and conflicts of opinion help to explain why, once again, Frenchmen are divided from the start in their attitudes towards a new régime. Their attitudes towards the Constitution are coloured by their reactions to the revolution that brought it into being. The second President of the Fourth Republic, M. Coty, described it as 'a necessary and a constructive revolution', as one that was 'effected in calm, and in respect for the very laws that had to be reformed'. This was true of the actual transition from the Fourth to the Fifth Republic. But the real revolution was by then over. Even though it was a bloodless one, even though it led to decisions that were taken in accordance with all the Constitutional and Parliamentary rules, and were ratified by the massive approval of the nation, it remains for many Frenchmen, by no means all on the Left, a revolution whose leaders were seeking to impose their will, in defiance of the Republican authorities. For a small minority on the Left the new régime represents a setback in the permanent battle for the victory of the Republican tradition; for some, it represents what they hope will be a temporary emergency; for others it represents an experiment in a Republican tradition different from that of the Fourth Republic.

CHAPTER III

The Nature of the Constitution

The Constitution of the Fifth Republic has been described as 'tailor-made for General de Gaulle', 'quasi-Monarchical,'[1] quasi-Presidential, a Parliamentary Empire, unworkable, 'the worst-drafted in French Constitutional history',[2] and ephemeral, to mention only a few of the French verdicts on it, almost all of which have been unflattering.

It is, in fact, a Constitution whose general characteristics are difficult to summarize, partly because the Constitutional text is, more than most, an incomplete description of the system of Government, partly because it is difficult to situate the Constitution politically in relation to its immediate predecessors. There has been a tendency on the part of writers, therefore, to single out one or more of its characteristics and label it accordingly—as Monarchist, Orléanist, Republican or Presidential. The truth is that it is a hybrid, an attempt to combine two constitutional principles, the possibility of whose peaceful co-existence has yet to be proved.

Uncertainty and confusion

Since all Constitutions are necessarily modified in practice, it is always unrealistic to base deductions about the nature of a régime

[1] v. for instance, M. Duverger's description of it as *Orléaniste* in *Revue française de Science Politique*, March 1959, and in *La Ve République* (Presses Universitaires de France, 1959).

[2] Quoted by R. Capitant in the preface to L. Hamon's *De Gaulle dans la République* (Plon, 1958).

solely on the provisions of written texts, though it is useful to study them as a help to understanding what the leaders of a new régime are trying to do. The Fifth Republic has made this task very difficult by omitting from the text of the Constitution of the 4th October provisions for a number of extremely important institutions. The electoral laws, for instance, the institutions of the Community, the composition and some of the rules of functioning of the two Houses of Parliament, the organization of the Judiciary, the functions of a number of organs such as the Economic and Social Council, the Higher Council of the Judiciary, as well as a number of other matters, are dealt with in a series of Ordinances, promulgated in no logical order, between October 1958 and February 1959. Some of these have the status of organic laws; in other words, a special legislative procedure is required to revise them; others are ordinary laws. Some deal with relatively trivial detail; others with questions of major importance. Some, in particular the Ordinances providing for the institutions of the Community, are themselves completed by Presidential '*décisions*', appearing from time to time in the *Journal Officiel*.

This is, then, to begin with, an untidy Constitution. It is also one which is in some places vague, and in others ambiguous. The difficulty of deciding the precise meaning of a number of articles is increased by the circumstances in which the Constitution was drawn up. That of the Fourth Republic was debated in Parliament for months, so that the precise shade of meaning given to this or that word, or article, by politicians of different parties was in no doubt and could be quoted later if difficulties of interpretation arose. The drafting of the Constitution of the Fifth Republic was the responsibility, not of Parliament but of the Government, and was done in private. A small Ministerial Committee presided over by General de Gaulle drew up a first draft which was approved by the Cabinet and then submitted to a Consultative Committee, mainly composed of Members of Parliament, and to the *Conseil d'Etat*, before being finally approved by the Cabinet. All that we have to go on is the Government's original text, the text as amended by the

Consultative Committee, and the final text, together with reports o
verbal explanations of some articles given in private session b
General de Gaulle. It is true that evidence of intention on the part o
the authors would not of itself confer constitutional authority an
that any Government remains free to adopt its own interpretatio
(except in the few specified cases where the Constitutional Council'
interpretation alone is valid). But where there is no judicial review
and where opinions are divided, evidence of intention can have con
siderable weight. The present Constitution is, more than mos
subject to varying interpretations on a number of points.[1]

There is, too, an additional difficulty in describing the institution
of the Fifth Republic. Some changes of régime have been muc
more wholesale than others. The Constitutions of both the Thir
and Fourth Republics left the administrative and judicial organi
zation of the country untouched. Indeed, local government organi
zation has changed very little during the present century and it i
often said that the general framework of French administratio
remains today much as it was under Napoleon. The Fifth Republi
set out to have a thorough spring-cleaning. Under the specia
powers conferred on the Government, first by Parliament and the
by Article 92 of the Constitution, over 300 Ordinances were pro
mulgated between June 1958 and February 1959. Some of the
deal with purely administrative matters, such as the reorganizatio
of the Paris markets, or of the medical service. Others provid
for profound changes, some of them long overdue. The organi
zation of national defence, of the Law Courts, the reform of crimina
procedure, Local Government reforms, including modifications o
the system of municipal elections, adminstrative changes affecting
Algeria and the Sahara, the status of Civil Servants, the radio—al
these, as they are applied, will modify considerably the admini
strative and judicial framework in which the new Constitution i
applied. Some will come into effect only slowly; some may neve

---

[1] Articles 5 and 16 are discussed in the chapter on the President, articles 3
and 37 in the chapter on Parliament, and articles 41 and 49 in the chapter or
the relations between Government and Parliament.

be applied at all. The Constitution of 1946 provided for changes in the organization of local Government that were, in fact, never carried out. But the provision, at least on paper, for all these changes, at a time when so many political and constitutional habits are also being changed, does intensify the atmosphere of uncertainty and confusion which surrounds the beginnings of the Fifth Republic.

Republican and Presidential characteristics

It has already been said that the Constitution is the expression of two very different, and probably conflicting, principles. The first is the principle of Republican Parliamentary government. The Constitution is in many ways a reaction against certain habits and institutions of the Fourth Republic, in particular those which are associated with what has been called in an earlier chapter the Left-wing Republican tradition. But it is nevertheless in many ways a Republican Constitution and, in accordance with the undertaking given by General de Gaulle's Government on taking office, it provides for a democratic and Parliamentary system of government. The head of the State and the head of the Government remain distinct. The Government is directed by the Prime Minister who appoints and dismisses his colleagues and is responsible to Parliament (in practice to the National Assembly only).[1] The two Houses of Parliament are democratically elected. The judiciary is independent.

The Constitution does seek, however, to reverse the tendency towards *gouvernement d'assemblée*, characteristic of the Fourth Republic, and indeed, deliberately encouraged by certain of the innovations of the Constitution of the Fourth Republic. Thus, the Senate's legislative powers are co-ordinate with those of the Assembly, except where the Government decides to give the Assembly the last word; Prime Ministers have both procedural and constitutional means of dominating the Assembly; and Parliament's rôle is

[1] But v. also pp. 145–7 on the powers exercised in practice by the President of the Republic.

both quantitatively and qualitatively diminished. Under the Fourth Republic, the Assembly was really in charge of legislation, the Government being obliged as a general rule to fight as best it could, for its Bills or its life, with the vote of confidence as almost its sole weapon.[1] Under the Fifth Republic, the Government is in charge of legislation, and even effective criticism by Parliament is difficult, unless the National Assembly is prepared to go to the length of defeating the Government.

Most of these changes do not imply any fundamental break with Republican tradition. They represent a reaction towards more right-wing tendencies than those that were mainly responsible for the 1946 Constitution. Some changes in Parliamentary procedure were also acceptable to elements on the Left, and had actually been included in proposals for Constitutional revision put forward in 1958. They are evidence of a desire on the part of some Parliamentarians, and in particular on the part of those who had held office under the Fourth Republic, to return to something nearer to the Parliamentary system as it functioned under the Third Republic. They are evidence, too, of a desire of many Gaullists to try to achieve Governmental stability by laying down strict Constitutional rules. It may be doubted whether either Constitutional or procedural rules can be an effective substitute for the unwritten agreement between Government and Opposition regarding the rules of the Parliamentary game, which is the real safeguard of Governmental stability and which, even more than the two-party system, explains the success of the British system. But that this was the intention of the authors of the Constitution is quite clear.[2]

One change, however, though not incompatible with Parliamentary government, is certainly in conflict with the Republican tradition, as it has been described in earlier pages. The 1958 Con-

---

[1] Prime Ministers of the Fourth Republic could dissolve the Assembly only in certain carefully defined circumstances, which in practice arose only once, in 1955.

[2] v. for instance, on this, M. Debré's speech to the *Conseil d'Etat* on 27th August 1958. (*Revue française de Science Politique*, March, 1959, pp. 7–29.)

stitution reverses the traditional relationship between the legislative and the rule-making authorities. Hitherto, though Parliament has always been free to delegate legislative powers to the Government, these have been 'special' powers, granted, and withdrawn, at the will of Parliament. The principle of the legislative supremacy of Parliament has remained intact. Henceforth, power to legislate is defined limitatively by the Constitution and, outside these limits, powers belong to the rule-making authority, that is to the Government.

The second principle, which might be described as that of personal leadership, is more than an innovation in French Republican Constitutions. It is a break with Republican tradition which has led some Frenchmen to fear that this Constitution may be misused in order to install some form of personal rule. A number of its provisions justify the description of being 'tailor-made for General de Gaulle' in at least three ways. General de Gaulle was himself largely responsible for their inclusion. His interpretation of their meaning will undoubtedly prevail, as long as he holds office. And the events described in the preceding chapter led both democrats and anti-democrats, Republicans and anti-Republicans to agree to their inclusion, with the essential difference that, in the minds of those faithful to Republican tradition, they were justified only by the emergency. They trusted him, as they would have trusted no-one else, not to misuse them. They trusted him all the more after the election to the Assembly of some 200 U.N.R. Deputies of whose political instincts they were profoundly suspicious. Since the emergency powers were conferred not only on General de Gaulle but also on any future President, they were anxious, however, lest at some time in the future, a President less scrupulous than General de Gaulle might interpret and use these powers for quite different ends.

The powers in question were first defended by General de Gaulle in 1946, in a speech at Bayeux. He then argued, first, that the head of the State should be a representative of the nation rather than of Parliament (that is, elected by a college larger than that consisting of the two Houses of Parliament) and that his functions should be those, not of an impartial figurehead, which is what Presidents of the Third and Fourth Republics usually were, but of a representative of the continuity of the State—an 'arbitrator' (*un arbitre*) 'above the accidents of political life'. As an arbitrator, he should, in normal circumstances, stand aloof from and above parties, and yet, at the same time, advise and guide Governments. Exactly how he could combine these two functions, the God-like and the human, has never been very clear and General de Gaulle is certainly the only man whom democratic Republicans would trust to succeed to do so.

This principle, of a President whose rôle is positive—who, though he does not govern, does more than reign—has been translated into practice in the 1958 Constitution by means of a division of executive power between President and Prime Minister that cannot be defined with precision. In normal circumstances, the President's function as an 'arbitrator' is intended to make him primarily an adviser of the Government. His real importance in the State, therefore, becomes an imponderable, a resultant of the impact on each other of the respective personalities of President and Prime Minister.

The nature of this impact during the first year or so of the Fifth Republic is discussed later.[1] All that needs to be noted here is the element both of confusion and uncertainty that this partial duality of the executive introduces. A President *may* remain in the background, as previous Presidents have done, using his new powers— the right to negotiate treaties, to dissolve the Assembly, to send messages to Parliament—in accordance with precedents, or on the advice of the Prime Minister. On the other hand, he may, as President de Gaulle has done, interpret these rights, or certain of them, in such a way as to lead him to govern, instead of reigning, in fields where responsibility for policy belongs constitutionally to the Prime Minister.

In one field, the theoretical possibilities of conflict seem very much greater. In his capacity as *ex-officio* President of the Com-

[1] *v. infra*, pp. 145–7.

munity, the President of the Republic is given explicit and extensive powers of decision, in a body—the Executive Council of the Community—in which the Prime Minister of France is represented ostensibly on the same footing as the Prime Ministers of the 12 other member-States. The various organic laws and decrees governing the organization of the Community are silent on the methods by which the policy of France (directed by the Prime Minister) and that of the Community (influenced, if not directed, by the President of the Community) can be harmonized, and the risk of Presidential split personality avoided.[1]

The Presidential functions mentioned up to now are exercised in normal circumstances. In times of national crisis, the President becomes even more important. In a grave national emergency, the head of the State should, in General de Gaulle's view, assume full powers.

> It must be his duty, if it should happen that the country fall into danger, to be the protector (*le garant*) of national independence, and of the treaties concluded by France.

The 1958 Constitution not only gives the President the right to exercise such powers. It also makes him both judge and jury, since he alone is constitutionally empowered to decide when such circumstances exist, and what measures are to be taken to restore normality.

Whether the two principles of Parliamentary government and Presidential leadership can co-exist in practice is a question that only the future can answer. Critics argue that, in abnormal circumstances, a President other than General de Gaulle could use these provisions to carry out a legal *coup d'état*, whilst, in normal circumstances, Republican and democratic opinion in France would find them intolerable and that the Constitution would, therefore, certainly be revised in order to eliminate them.

---

[1] On this, *v. infra*, pp. 158–161.

The incompatibility rule

The third important innovation in the 1958 Constitution which is certainly in conformity with General de Gaulle's views is the separation of legislative and executive powers, including the rule making Ministerial office incompatible with membership of Parliament. As expressed in 1946 and since, General de Gaulle's argument is that:

> It goes without saying that executive power should not emanate from Parliament—a Parliament which should be bi-cameral and should exercise legislative power—or the result will be a confusion of powers which will reduce the Government to a mere conglomeration of delegations. . . . The unity, cohesion and internal discipline of the French Government must be held sacred, if national leadership is not to degenerate rapidly into incompetence and impotence.
>
> But how, in the long run, can this unity, this cohesion and this discipline be maintained if executive power is the emanation of the very power that it ought to counter-blance, and if each member of a Government that is collectively responsible to the representatives of the whole nation conducts himself, in his Ministerial post, as the delegate of a party?

To British minds, this argument is unconvincing and unrealistic. And it must be added that it also fails to convince large sections of French opinion. But on this issue there is no clear-cut division of opinion between orthodox Republicans and supporters of a Presidential, or quasi-Presidential system. Though French Republican Constitutions have traditionally rejected the right of the judiciary to intervene in disputes between the citizen and the administration, and also judicial review of the constitutionality of legislation, there has never been the same degree of unanimity regarding the separation of executive and legislative functions.

Governments of both the Third and Fourth Republics were normally made up of members of Parliament. But it was not unusual

or a Government to include Ministers who were not. Indeed Léon
Blum's Government in 1936 included three women Under-Secre-
taries though women were not then eligible for membership of
either House. War-time and post-war Governments included non-
Parliamentary 'technicians' from time to time. Since French
Ministers are, by virtue of their office, entitled to attend and speak
in either House (though not, of course, to vote, except in the House
of which they are members) these exceptions did not create the kind
of difficulty which arises in England when a Minister holding important office is not a Member of the House of Commons. Some
previous Republican Constitutions, however, have made governmental office incompatible with membership of Parliament.[1] And
during the discussions on the Constitution that preceded the 1958
Referendum, the majority of the Socialist Parliamentary group and
also of the party's *comité directeur* expressed their approval of the
incompatibility rule.

On the other hand, there was opposition to it on both the Right
and the Left. The Consultative Constitutional Committee, for instance, suggested an amendment to the rules, as formulated in the
Government's draft Constitution, which, in effect, constituted
a repudiation of the principle.[2]

Other claims to originality

(a) PARTIES. In addition to its quasi-Presidential aspects, the 1958
Constitution includes three innovations in particular justifying its
description as being in a category of its own—*hors série*. The first

[1] *v.* for example, 1791 (*Titre* III, Chapter 1, Section III, articles 3 and 4),
1793 (Girondine) (*Titre* III, Section III, article 25), 1795, (articles 47 and 136).
[2] The amendment proposed (*a*) that (in conformity with traditional practice)
Ministers should be chosen either from inside or outside Parliament; and (*b*)
that during their period of office they should cease to be members of political
parties, should engage in no party-political activities and should be suspended
from membership of Parliament. Unless the intention was to sabotage the
incompatibility rule, this seems a pointless gesture. In virtually all cases
Ministers' political opinions would be known and their eventual return to
party politics taken for granted.

is its explicit recognition (in Article 4) of the rôle of political parties. For the first time, a Republican Constitution not merely mentions parties, but acknowledges them as a normal constituent of political life. During his 12 years in the political wilderness, General de Gaulle's public utterances usually included attacks on them. Under the Fifth Republic, the formation of parties and their freedom of action are constitutionalized, on one condition. They are required ' to respect the principles of national sovereignty and democracy'. This article is generally assumed to be intended less to encourage the formation of democratic parties than to make it possible for the Communist party, whose loyalty to France and respect for democracy are not generally apparent, to be banned, should necessity arise.[1] But whatever the ulterior motives, the article does, at least implicitly, make legal imposition of one-party government unconstitutional and, explicitly, make respect for democracy a constitutional requirement.

(b) THE CONSTITUTIONAL COUNCIL. Though the 1958 Constitution does not provide for anything that could be described as judicial review, it does create a body which, within certain specific and narrowly defined limits, has the function of deciding on the constitutionality of Governmental or Parliamentary acts. The Constitutional Council replaces the Constitutional Committee, set up by the 1946 Constitution with the very restricted function of pronouncing on the constitutionality of any Bill challenged conjointly, on that ground, by a majority of the Senate and the President of the Republic. It was called on to act only once, and then on a relatively minor technical matter.

The Constitutional Council's rôle is more important. It has four distinct functions. First, it supervises the regularity of the elections of the President of the Republic and of referenda, announces the results, is responsible for declaring the Presidency vacant if for any

[1] In fact, the Government was able to ban the Communist party altogether in 1939, and in Algeria since the outbreak of the rebellion, without the aid of such an article. Its value, other than as a declaration of principle, is, therefore, problematical.

cause the President cannot carry out his duties, and decides cases in which the regularity of Parliamentary elections is contested. Second, it *must* be consulted on the conformity with the Constitution of organic laws and the Standing Orders of both Houses. The Council merely pronounces on the question of constitutionality, leaving the Government or Parliament, as the case may be, to take the appropriate steps to regularize the situation. Its decision is final. Third, it acts as an advisory body to the President if he is contemplating the assumption of emergency powers. It *must* be consulted by him regarding both the existence of such an emergency (on which its opinion, with reasons, must be published) and the measures that he proposes to take to deal with it. But the President is not constitutionally obliged to accept its advice. Fourth, the Council's ruling *may* be sought by the President, the Prime Minister, or the President of either House as to the conformity with the Constitution of an international agreement or a law about to be promulgated (other than an organic law, on which it must be consulted) and on certain conflicts which may arise between the Government and Parliament regarding the delimitation of executive and legislative competence.

The Council has no general responsibility for ensuring respect for the Constitution. It can express its opinion only if consulted on the matters enumerated above and on the initiative of the persons mentioned. It has no power to enforce its decisions. If President, Government and Parliament were to agree to refrain from consulting the Council on a matter where consultation is optional, then there is no means by which the Council can make its views known. The citizen cannot appeal to it nor can any Courts of Law. It is not, therefore, in any sense comparable to the Supreme Court of the United States.

Nevertheless, on matters on which it must be, or is, in fact, con-consulted, the Council may have great influence in determining the interpretation to be placed on certain ambiguous provisions of the Constitution.[1]

[1] *v.* for instance, the Council's first decision, which is discussed on p. 120. The Council consists of nine members, appointed in equal numbers by the

(c) THE COMMUNITY. The concept of the Community, its organization and prospects, will be discussed in more detail in a later chapter. It is perhaps relevant, however, at this stage, to emphasize the fact that the 1958 Constitution is the first one in French history to abandon explicitly (except in the case of the four Overseas *départements* and five small Overseas Territories) the assimilationist principle that has dominated French thinking in this field since the Revolution. It opens the way to a relationship between Madagascar and 12 African Territories on the one hand and the French Republic (including, at the moment, Algeria, the Sahara and the Overseas *départements* and Territories) on the other which is intended to be something between a Federation and a Commonwealth; a relationship which the Constitution declares to be susceptible of further evolution, not excluding independence for any member, on terms negotiated with France. The word 'independent' is used for the first time in this context in a French Constitution, with reference to the organization of former overseas dependencies.

The originality of these provisions does not lie merely in the proposal for some kind of federal relationship—an objective which was already that of General de Gaulle in 1946:

> The future of the 110 million men and women under our flag, (he said in his Bayeux speech) lies in a federal form of organization that time will determine little by little, but whose beginning must be recognized and whose development must be provided for, in our new Constitution. (That is, the 1946 Constitution.)

It lies also in the methods provided for in the 1958 Constitution for implementing the promise of evolution. By 1956, the evolution of the Overseas Territories had gone beyond anything contem-

President of the Republic and the Presidents of the two Houses. Councillors sit for nine years and are not eligible for a second term. Former Presidents of the Republic are members *ex officio* for life. The President of the Republic appoints the President of the Council from among its members. The President does not require a counter-signature in making these appointments.

lated, or even authorized, ten years earlier, on a strict reading of the Constitution. In the view of some Frenchmen, the 'outline-law' of 1956 could be regarded as constitutional only by a somewhat generous interpretation of the provisions of Title VIII of the Constitution and any further evolution was impossible without a revision of this section, which governed the organization of the Overseas Territories. The new Constitution specifically lays down that any future change of status of the member States of the new Community, even one involving the grant of independence, can be made without the need to revise the Constitution. It may well be that the retention by the President of important powers of decision in the organs of the Community reflects as well as his confidence in his own ability to adapt to the rapidly evolving situation in Africa, his determination not to allow reforms granted on paper to be sabotaged in practice by administrative or political conservatism, as has so frequently happened in the course of French colonial history and in the history of Franco-Algerian relations.

Advisory and Judicial organs

Of the two advisory bodies set up under the 1946 Constitution, the Assembly of the Union and the Economic Council, only the latter survives, under the title of the Economic and Social Council. Both its composition and its functions are somewhat changed.[1]

[1] The Economic Council consists of 205 members, chosen for five years by appropriate professional organizations, or by the Government, to represent the following interests and areas:

45, manual and black-coated workers,
41, private and nationalized industry and commercial concerns,
40, agriculture,
20, Algeria and the Sahara,
10, the Overseas *départements*,
10, economic and social interests Overseas,
15, various economic, social and cultural interests,
15, various social activities, including housing, co-operatives, family associations,
7, various special interests,
2, the middle classes.

Its field of advice is now to be restricted to matters on which it is consulted by the Government, except for any suggestions it may make regarding either social and economic reforms necessitated by technical changes, or the Republic's contribution to the economic and social development of the community. Under the Fourth Republic, it was free to study and report on any matters within its field of competence and could be consulted by the Assembly as well as by the Government. Its sessions are no longer to be public and much of its work will be done in Technical Sections, to which outside specialists are co-opted. These changes indicate that the Fifth Republic intends to use the Council primarily as a technical adviser. Under the Fourth Republic, its debates were often influenced by political considerations and it often divided along orthodox political lines.

The Higher Council of the Judiciary remains, but also with restricted functions and somewhat different methods of appointment. Its function is to advise the Government on appointments (but only to certain of the higher judicial posts), to act as disciplinary Court for judges, and also to advise the President on his exercise of the right of pardon. Henceforth, it is consulted as of right, on questions of reprieve, only where the death sentence is in question. Under the Fourth Republic it was also responsible for ensuring the independence of judges and for the general organization of Courts of Law. These functions now return to the Ministry of Justice.[1]

The purpose of the Fourth Republic in handing over these last-mentioned functions to the Higher Council had been to prevent political influence in promotions. Complaints began to be heard, however, alleging political bias in some appointments by the Higher

[1] The Higher Council of the Judiciary is composed of nine members, sitting for four years and eligible for a second term only. They are appointed by the President of the Republic (with the counter-signature of the Prime Minister). The President of the Republic and the Minister of Justice are members *ex officio*, the former acting as President, the latter as Vice-President. Seven of the nine members are chosen from different branches of the legal profession from lists submitted by the relevant directing bodies.

Council and some overlapping with the Ministry of Justice. Under the special powers granted to the Government by the Constitution from October 1958 to February 1959, a number of Ordinances and Decrees provided for a comprehensive reorganization of criminal procedure, for redistribution of Law Courts, and for improvements in the status and training of judges, designed to improve their quality. It will be some years before these reforms can be completed.

The function of the High Court of Justice is, as it was under the Fourth Republic, to try Presidents of the Republic on a charge of high treason, and Ministers on charges under the penal code, provided that the offences were punishable at the time they were committed. It also tries Ministers and their accomplices on charges of plotting against the safety of the State. To bring individuals before it, both Houses must pass identical motions by an absolute majority of their members. The vote is public.

The only changes of importance in the method of functioning of the Court are, first, that decisions to bring an individual before the Court must now be taken by both Houses instead of by the National Assembly alone, as was the position under the Fourth Republic; second, that the vote is no longer secret, and, third, that the sentence on a President of the Republic found guilty of high treason (the only offence with which he can be charged in the exercise of his functions) is no longer to be determined on the basis of rules laid down in the penal code. This requirement is retained, however, in the case of all other offenders dealt with by the High Court.[1]

Constitutional revision

Like the 1946 Constitution, that of 1958 includes a special procedure for revision. It is relatively simple—simple that is, as far as the

---

[1] The High Court of Justice is composed of 24 members, 12 chosen by each House from among their members, following a general election in the case of Deputies, and a partial renewal in the case of Senators. They hold office until the following election or partial renewal.

D

constitutional requirements are concerned, though not necessaril
politically easy to apply. A proposal for revision (which can com
either from the President of the Republic, at the suggestion of th
Prime Minister, or from private Members) must, to be effective, b
voted first in identical terms by both Houses or Parliament and the
ratified by a Referendum, or, if the President decides otherwise, b
a two-thirds majority of both Houses, sitting together as a Congress.
The Republican form of government is not subject to revision.

It remains to be seen whether these conditions will be met mor
easily than those governing revision under the 1946 Constitution
Under the Fourth Republic, the operative requirement which en
abled the Assembly, if necessary, to dispense with the consent of th
Senate was a two-thirds majority in the National Assembly, a con
dition that the National Assembly was frequently unable to fulfi
Under the Fifth Republic the Senate has an effective veto and th
first stage of revision may, therefore, be more difficult to complete.

[1] Revision of the articles of *Titre* XII (the Community) constitutes a
exception, requiring only ordinary legislation. Such laws must be voted, how
ever, in the same terms by the Senate of the Community.

[2] It has been suggested by M. Duverger (*v. Revue française de Scien
Politique*, March 1959, pp. 138–9) that the wording of the article governin
revision (article 89) is ambiguous in that it does not make clear wheather th
President's decision not to submit a proposed revision to a Referendu
renders the first stage (a vote in both Houses) unnecessary, or is taken onl
subsequent to its having been completed. Both logically and linguistically th
second interpretation seems the only acceptable one. M. Duverger also raise
the question as to whether the President can decide not to hold a Referendu
only in the case of proposals made by the Government, or whether the origi
of the proposals is immaterial once the proposals have been voted in bot
Houses. The use, at this stage, of the word *projet* only would support th
first interpretation.

There are also a number of other ambiguities. The article gives no informa
tion regarding the procedure governing the 'voting' of a proposal for revisio
Article 126 of the Standing Orders makes it clear that the ordinary legislativ
procedure will be used, but it is still not clear whether the procedure is th
same in Congress as in the two Houses.

The conflict of constitutional objectives

The attempt to combine the two principles of Parliamentary and Presidential government constitutes the specifically Gaullist element in the 1958 Constitution, whether or not General de Gaulle was himself personally responsible for the formulation of any of its provisions. But those who drafted the Constitution were responsible for at least three other influences which left their mark.

The two former Prime Ministers who were members of the Ministerial drafting Committee were left-wing Republicans who had really two aims. The first was to produce a democratic Constitution, preserving the essential principles of traditional Republican and Parliamentary government. Neither had any real quarrel with the principles of the 1946 Constitution, in the drafting of which M. Mollet had certainly taken an active part. Both were preoccupied, however, by the practical difficulties that they had encountered in trying to govern in the conditions which prevailed throughout most of the life of the Fourth Republic. M. Pflimlin's Government had succeeded in introducing proposals for constitutional revision, intended to strengthen Governments, but the Fourth Republic fell before they had become law. The essentials of these proposals were, therefore, included in the 1958 Constitution.

No doubt, in their Ministerial capacity, left-wing Ministers of the Fourth Republic could welcome, too, the reduction of Parliamentary sessions to five and a half months. The practical objective of most French Prime Ministers since the war has been well described as that of persuading Deputies to take long vacations, an objective often achieved under the Third Republic by the system of *décrets-lois*, though not under the Fourth, which had to rely on devices such as special powers Acts and the practice of legislation in the form of outline-laws. The ex-Ministers and their party supporters are less likely to appreciate the restrictions now that they have gone into opposition.[1]

[1] The Socialist party's adherence to the principle of Parliamentary sovereignty has, in practice, led to a tendency to favour *gouvernement d'assemblée* and the Catholic M.R.P. which is in many ways very close to the Socialists,

They fitted in very well, however, with the conceptions of th
Minister of Justice, M. Debré, who was responsible for organizin
the work of the Ministerial committee and for drawing up the work
ing-draft. There is considerable evidence to suggest that the 195
Constitution owes more to M. Debré than to anyone else.[1] He ha
spent fifteen years, beginning in the underground resistance move
ment, working out the Constitutional reforms that would hel
to give France the kind of Government she needed. It prob
ably owes to him some of the most unworkable of its provi
sions—the effort to constitutionalize procedure, for instance, an
to define and limit the sphere of activity of Parliament by rigi
rules, described by one legal expert as 'the pure and simple organi
zation of anarchy'.[2]

M. Debré shares neither the revolutionary inheritance nor th
Parliamentary outlook of the left-wing Ministers. He is a loya
Gaullist, an inexperienced Minister and an unskilled Parliamentary
performer, an intelligent and precise lawyer and a highly respectec
Conseiller d'Etat, a doctrinaire reformer and a frustrated pedagogue
His aim was to discipline Deputies and, by showing them who wa:
master, lead them to a better way of life.

Lastly, there is discernible in the Constitution the faint protest
the sigh of regret, of orthodox, mainly right-wing, Republican anc
Parliamentary opinion, represented by members of the Constitu
tional Advisory Committee, presided over by M. Paul Reynaud
Whatever their feelings about the political situation in 1958, anc
its necessities, their spiritual home remained the Parliamentary
traditions of the immediately preceding régimes.

has a similar outlook. It was however, an M.R.P. Minister—M. Lecourt, a
former Minister of Justice—who was primarily responsible for the comple>
proposals whose essential purpose was realized in article 49. They owe littl
to theory and practically everything to the hard school of ministerial experience

[1] *v.* the excellent piece of research on this subject in *Revue française d*
Science Politique, March 1959, by Nicholas Wahl, *Aux Origines de la Nouvelle*
Constitution.

[2] G. Morange, *La hiérarchie des textes dans la Constitution du 4 octobre*
1958 (*Recueil Dalloz hebdomadaire*, 28th January 1959, p. 26).

These four schools of thought were all, to some extent, looking backwards. General de Gaulle had never forgotten 1940 and was anxious that in any future national emergency the continuity of the State should be better provided for than it had been then. The left-wing Ministers wanted stronger Republican Governments than they had headed under the Fourth Republic. M. Debré wanted to make a new place for Parliament and to see that it kept to it, and the members of Parliament whose advice was sought on the new Constitution were trying to salvage what remnants they could of the Parliamentary rights and habits of the Third Republic.

The result was a Constitution whose provisions are often ambiguous or obscure and whose purposes are sometimes confused and contradictory. It is ironical that one of the chief victims is likely to be the Prime Minister himself, since the duality of the Executive resulted in the spectacle of the first Prime Minister, M. Debré, playing understudy to the first President, and often apparently working from a different edition of his part. In the long series of French Constitutions, that of 1958 is unlikely to be remembered as a model of either the logic or the clarity of thought and expression on which the French (often rightly) pride themselves.

CHAPTER IV

The Electoral System and French Electoral Habits

Electoral stability and instability

It is a prevalent British opinion that the French are addicted to systems of proportional representation, that their electoral behaviour is characterized by great fickleness, and that an electoral system designed to discourage the formation of small splinter parties would do a great deal to cure the Governmental instability from which France has suffered since the beginning of the Third Republic. In fact, except for a brief period in 1945 and 1946, France has never had fully proportional representation and all the evidence shows that, at least up to the end of the second world war, French electorates presented a striking picture of stability. Studies of electoral behaviour have shown, not only that the overall electoral strength of certain basic political tendencies varied very little up to 1939, but that in certain regions political convictions remained surprisingly consistent for nearly a century. André Siegfried noted this fact in 1930:

> The same political orientation, expressed by virtually the same majorities, can be found often in a *département* or a *canton* over a period of fifty years or more. Beneath changing political labels

that deceive the superficial observer, these fundamental tendencies constitute a solid basis for political evolution.[1]

François Goguel estimated that, between 1877 and 1928, the relative strengths of what he termed the forces of movement and those of order, or what are usually referred to more loosely as the forces of Left and Right, varied by only 0·5 per cent.[2]

General stability of opinion is not, of course, inconsistent with changes in the electoral complexion of certain regions. These are often due to changes in economic structure, changes which, over the country as a whole, often cancel each other out. Nor is it inconsistent with considerable fluctuations in the number of seats held by different parties or tendencies, often brought about by changes in the electoral system, or by electoral alliances affecting the working of electoral systems. For if Frenchmen have tended to stick to their principles or their parties in successive elections, they have certainly not stuck to one system of election. Between 1875 and 1958 France changed her electoral system eight times. And of the five different systems used during that period, only one was used for more than two successive elections. Of the 22 elections between 1875 and 1958, however, only three were conducted on a wholly proportional system, and they all took place between October 1945 and November 1946.

Nor does a study of French electoral systems in relation to party or governmental instability bear out the thesis that the electoral system has encouraged instability. The elections of 1924, 1936 and 1946, for instance, were held on different systems. All resulted in

---

[1] *Tableau des Partis en France* (Grasset, 1930), p. 52.

[2] *La Politique des Partis sous la IIIe République* (Paris, Editions du Seuil, 1946), p. 20.

Cf. also R. Aron in *Preuves* (February 1959, p. 9): '75 per cent of the French who voted in November and December 1958 were faithful to their traditional preferences. They were almost as stable as British electors, 10 per cent of whom, by changing their party, can bring the Labour revolution or a Conservative return to power. The difference is that France changes her régime or her Constitution and that, within the Parliamentary system, the French vote for so many parties that they give a mandate to none.'

large majorities for left-wing coalitions yet in every case the coalition had broken down long before the end of the Parliament.[1]

What does seem generally true of French electoral systems is first, that, except for the brief period following the war, during which proportional representation was tried, they have been deliberately designed to produce some degree of disproportion between votes and seats, with the aim either of reducing the number of small and undisciplined splinter groups, or of obtaining, in spite of them, an Assembly in which there would be a coherent majority, or sometimes with the specific aim of reducing Communist, or Communist and Gaullist representation. In two elections, those of 1919 and 1924, the system chosen was intended to produce gross distortion, and did so.[2] That introduced in the elections of 1951 was intended to reduce Communist and Gaullist representation.

[1] In case this example should be taken to justify the thesis that left-wing Governments are more unstable than right, the following examples could also be quoted: from 1917–24 right-centre Governments had an average life of eleven months; from 1924–8 and 1936–40 left-wing or left-centre Governments had an average life of eight months; from 1946–51 centre-left coalitions (for the most part excluding the Communists) had an average life of seven and a half months; from 1951–55 centre-right coalitions had an average life of eight months; and from 1956–8 centre-left coalitions had an average life of about eight and a half months. The electoral system that produced the 1924 Chamber was different from that of 1936; that of 1946 differed from that of 1951.

It has been estimated that, between 1919 and 1957, the average life of Governments was six and a half months during Assemblies elected by proportional, or quasi-proportional, systems and five months during those elected by majority systems (v. M. Massenet, *L'Angoisse au Pouvoir*, Plon, 1959, p. 5).

[2] The 1919 system was a hybrid. Candidates stood either as individuals or as members of lists, and electors had as many votes as there were seats to be filled, though they were not obliged to use them all. They could not give more than one vote to a single candidate, but they could vote for candidates on different lists. The *département* was usually the constituency. Seats were allocated in three stages. Candidates receiving an absolute majority of the votes cast were elected. Remaining seats were allocated, first proportionally, by the application of a quotient, but with preference given to list candidates, any further vacant seats going to the list with the highest average. The result was a gross over-representation of majorities.

This it did, producing in 1951 considerable disproportion between votes and seats. In 1956, however, it produced much less disproportion, owing to changes in party structures, and still more in party alliances.[1]

French electoral systems and the numerous proposals for electoral reform that have been put forward since the war also reveal a distinct preference in the minds of many politicians for involved systems. In 1951 eight, and in 1955 11 different proposals were debated in the Assembly, a number of them highly complicated and ingenious combinations of majority or proportional principles, with one or more ballots and list or individual voting.

Finally, the French are deeply divided about the electoral system itself. It has been said that what they are looking for is:

> a system that would produce assemblies that accurately reflected the divisions of the electorate and parties that were stable, disciplined and responsible. Experience has shown that in France an electoral system can yield the first result but not the second.[2]

[1] The 1951 system was also a hybrid. Voting was for party lists at a single ballot, any list receiving an absolute majority of the votes cast in the constituency taking all the seats. Parties could also form alliances, which were announced on the ballot paper. Allied lists took all the seats if they received an absolute majority of the votes cast, allocation between them being proportional to the number of votes received. Where no list, or group of lists, received an absolute majority, allocation of seats was proportional, but the allied group still counted as a single list for this purpose, the system being one which over-represented large blocks of votes; within the group the allocation of seats was proportional to votes received. In 1951, alliances between non-Communist and non-Gaullist parties effectively reduced the representation of the former, though the latter did well. In 1956, the Gaullists had virtually disappeared and the multiplicity of alliances prevented all but 11 alliances from obtaining an absolute majority. The result was, therefore, much closer to proportional representation.

[2] Peter Campbell, *French Electoral Systems and Elections 1789-1957* (Faber, 1958), p. 45. The first part of this excellent study provides a well-documented refutation of the thesis that the electoral system is responsible for political instability.

Experience has also shown that political divisions prevented any serious or prolonged attempt to achieve one of the above results at the cost of sacrificing the other. Electoral systems have been either designed to meet a particular emergency or to produce a particular result, in which case they have been speedily abandoned once the conditions responsible for their creation ceased to exist, or else they have been compromises in which electoral principles have been adapted in order to meet the requirements of majority parties with conflicting electoral interests. No system has succeeded in satisfying a sufficient number of politicians for long enough to enable the problem to be removed from the field of political controversy. Sooner or later, those who lost by the system have wanted to change it.

This electoral instability has itself contributed both to Parliamentary deadlock and to Governmental instability. Assembly and Government have at times wanted to change the system, but have been powerless to do so, owing to party divisions on the electoral issue. Yet it is only natural that parties should oppose the adoption of systems whose effect would be to weaken them. The Catholic M.R.P. and the Communist party have always believed that they fare better under a system of proportional representation than under one involving alliances, for the latter is isolated, and the former finds that Socialist parties in some constituencies are reluctant to ally themselves with a clerical party. The Right, traditionally indisciplined and liable to form small, often ephemeral, groups, has tended to fear both proportional representation and the single-member system with two ballots, since it has been at a disadvantage compared with large disciplined parties. It has tended, therefore, to prefer one of the more complex systems, involving both majority and proportional systems and allowing a good deal of free play for manoeuvre within the constituency. The Socialists have been divided, being attracted in principle to the proportional system, but conscious of their need of alliances in practice. The Radicals have remained faithful to the single-member system with two ballots, which is associated *par excellence* with the Third Republic, when the Radical party was at its peak.

French electoral habits since the war have differed from those of the Third Republic in two major ways. First the distribution of votes between the traditional parties has changed. It is no longer true to say that the average French elector votes Radical. This party, which dominated the Third Republic's political life, is now both small and divided. Whereas, in 1932, over 19 per cent of the votes were cast for the Radical party, in 1946 the proportion was only 13 per cent, in 1956 13·5 per cent, in 1958 11 per cent, divided between three different tendencies. There has been a move to the Left on the part of the electors. This tendency was already observable before the war. The Radical party was then losing ground to the Socialists. During the year following the war, the Socialist party reached its peak, with almost 18 per cent of the votes. But the victory was short-lived, for the real shift of opinion was farther left. In 1946 the Communist vote reached 28·6 per cent, and, until 1958, Communist strength was consistently in the region of 25 per cent.[1]

The second change is the appearance of a high percentage of apparently floating voters. In 1945, the M.R.P. (*Mouvement Républicain Populaire*), a progressive Catholic party formed during the resistance period, polled 4¾ million votes. In 1946, with 5½ million votes, it became the largest party, polling nearly half a million more votes than the Communists. In the following election, a few months later, the Communists moved up to first place and by 1951 the M.R.P. vote had fallen to 2¼ million. It has since remained at round about that figure. The position of second largest party was filled in 1951 by another newcomer, the Gaullist R.P.F. (*Rassemblement du Peuple Français*), founded in 1947. This movement polled over 4 million votes. By 1956 it had disappeared. A small Gaullist rump polled something under a million votes and a third newcomer, the extreme Right Poujadist movement, received over 2½ million

---

[1] It is often stated that a quarter of the French electorate votes for the Communist party. This has never been true. From 1946 to 1958 about one elector in five and one voter in four did so. About 75 per cent to 80 per cent of the French electorate normally vote.

votes. In the 1958 election, the Poujadist and extreme Right vote together amounted to only about half a million, but a new formation —Gaullist, in the sense that its members acknowledge General de Gaulle as their leader, though he himself has no direct links with them and forbade any party to use his name in the electoral campaign —polled 3½ million votes.

The rise of four new formations attracting between an eighth and a quarter of the total vote, and the fall of three of them, all within the space of 13 years, during which six elections were held, does not seem to indicate a high degree of electoral stability. Yet in a sense it does. Although these four movements represent a great many different, and sometimes conflicting, political tendencies, they do have something in common. The extremist tendency which is present in at least three of the four movements has been a recurrent phenomenon in Republican France. The eighties saw the Boulangist movement. The first decade of the twentieth century saw extreme nationalist movements, of which the most important was the *Action Française*. The thirties saw the formation of a number of para-military groups with views ranging from corporatism to Fascism and tactics ranging from anti-Parliamentarianism to the terrorism of the *Cagoulards*. The fifties again saw the formation of extreme Right groups. The electoral strength of most of these was negligible, because, as opponents of the Parliamentary system, they often refused to take part in elections.

Those who voted for the four above-mentioned formations also included many who could not be classed as anti-Republican or anti-Parliamentary. They had in common a certain dissatisfaction with traditional political parties, a desire for something new. Three of the formations (not the M.R.P.) also expressed dissatisfaction with the system of Parliamentary government under the Fourth Republic. In other words, there has been in post-war France a consistently high 'disgruntlement' vote. On the Left, it tends to be cast in favour of the Communist party; on the Right, or among the non-politically minded, it tends to be cast for new formations, either attacking the 'system', or looking to personal leadership, or both.

The present electoral system

(a) THE NATIONAL ASSEMBLY. Though, by 1955, there was general agreement that the electoral law of 1951 ought to be revised, political divisions and conflicting electoral interests prevented the revision from being achieved during the life of the Fourth Republic. The new régime took the matter out of the hands of Parliament. The Constitution gave the Government full powers, until 5th February 1959, to legislate by Ordinances having the force of law, and specifically authorized it to determine the electoral system. This does not mean that Parliament's traditional right to vote and revise the electoral laws has been lost. On the contrary, electoral laws are included among the matters enumerated in article 34 of the Constitution as belonging to the legistative sphere. But until Parliament decides to change it, the electoral system laid down in the *Ordonnance* of 13th October 1958 remains that of the Fifth Republic.

That system is, for elections to the National Assembly, the single-member system with two ballots, the simplest of all French systems and the one which had been used for 13 of the 21 previous elections. Though this choice is reported to have been made by General de Gaulle himself, it was not popular with the Gaullists, who preferred a majority system with list voting and two ballots, as being more likely to favour a large and (for the time being) united party. The single-member system with two ballots is not used, however, for the election of all the 552 Deputies of the National Assembly. In all four systems are used:

(i) In the 90 *départements* of France and Corsica, 465 Deputies, and in the four Overseas *départements* ten Deputies are elected on this system.[1]

(ii) The five Overseas Territories elect six Deputies. Four

[1] The four Overseas *départements* are Guadeloupe, Martinique, Réunion and Guyana.

constitute single-member constituencies, the fifth a two
member constituency. There is one ballot only.[1]

(iii) Algeria elects 67 Deputies, of whom 46 are required to b
Moslem and 21 European or assimilated Moslems.[2] In eac
of 18 constituencies, parties present lists including Moslem
and European candidates in proportions decided on th
basis of the population, though not in proportion to th
relative strengths of the two communities. There is on
ballot only, and any list receiving a relative majority i
declared elected. Electors, whether European or Moslem
can vote only for a whole list.[3]

(iv) The two Saharan *départements* of Oasis and Saoura elec
four Deputies. Saoura elects one; in Oasis voting is for list
of three candidates. In both *départements*, candidates can b
either European or Moslem.

To be elected on the single-member system with two ballots, a
candidate must obtain either a minimum of 50 per cent plus 1 o
the votes cast at the first ballot, and a number of votes equal to a
quarter of the electorate, or head the poll at a second ballot held a
week later.[4]

In metropolitan France, in 1958, only 39 of the 465 candidate
were elected at the first ballot. Traditionally, during the perio
between the two ballots, discussions are carried on between th
parties contesting the election, with a view to deciding whether al

[1] The five Overseas Territories are St Pierre-et-Miquelon, Somaliland, Nev
Caledonia, Polynesia and the Comoro archipelago. The last-mentioned is a
two-member constituency.

[2] On the distinction between Moslems and Europeans *v. infra*, p. 175 n.1.

[3] The Algerian electorate numbered 4¼ million, in 1958, of whom 3½ millio
were Moslems. Moslem candidates were generally in the proportion of thre
to two, that is one European for every 35,000 Europeans and one Moslem fo
every 75,000 Moslem electors. The disproportion was much greater unde
earlier régimes.

[4] Elections in France are held on Sundays. Exceptionally in 1956, when th
election followed a dissolution, they were held on a Monday in order to avoi
their being held on New Year's Day.

andidates shall stand again, or whether one or more shall stand down, either retiring and leaving the field clear for the others, or etiring with the recommendation that supporters shall vote for one pecified candidate among those left. In pre-war elections, the econd ballot sometimes became a straight fight between Right and Left. Radicals, Socialists and Communists sometimes concluded greements to the effect that two of the three party representatives hould stand down in favour of the one who polled most votes at he first ballot. Sometimes the agreement was tacit or partial only. Since the elector was free to ignore the advice given, there was never any absolute guarantee that such undertakings would be honoured. In pre-war elections, too, it was possible for new candidates to intervene at the second ballot and this could put all the calculations out. This is now forbidden.

The general conditions governing the eligibility of candidates and the qualifications of electors are the same whatever the electoral ystem used.[1] All electors must be French, over 21 and in possession of their civil and political rights.[2] Their names must be included in he electoral register and, in *communes* of over 5,000, they must produce satisfactory proof of their identity to officials in the polling booths. They may not vote in more than one constituency. If they

---

[1] In 1958 there were some differences, both in the conditions governing candidatures and in voting practice in Algeria. Owing to the backwardness of he country and the need to protect voters from reprisals threatened by the F.L.N. (which boycotted the election) the army was in control of the arrangements and elections were staggered over three days, to enable elections to be held in safety. Moslem electors, most of whom are illiterate, voted by means of coloured cards and there were special polling booths in some areas for Moslem women, who were voting for the first time. Civilian control commissions had representatives in each constituency, to supervise the regularity of the elections. There were, nevertheless, criticisms of the army's conduct of affairs and allegations of political propaganda by the army, though General de Gaulle had issued specific instructions that everything was to be done to enable all political tendencies to express themselves freely.

[2] Among those disqualified are certain categories of the insane, declared bankrupts, those convicted of certain penal offences . . . etc. Some sentences pecifically disqualify the person convicted from voting.

can qualify as electors in more than one constituency, they must choose to be registered in one only. Postal votes are permitted for certain specified categories (the ill and aged, for instance, commercial travellers, lighthouse keepers, servicemen away from home . . . etc.). Proxy votes are permitted in the case of servicemen overseas, and of officials or French citizens resident abroad.

Candidates are elected for five years. They must be French and over 23. They may not stand in more than one constituency.[1] They are required to pay a deposit of 100,000 francs, which is reimbursed if they receive 5 per cent of the votes in either ballot.[2] They also have the right to a certain amount of free publicity, or rather the cost of this publicity is reimbursed to those who obtain 5 per cent of the votes cast. It includes posters on official hoardings and the printing and postage of election addresses and election cards. The purpose of this concession is to provide something like equality between candidates. In theory, no other posters or correspondence are permitted. In practice, this rule is easily evaded. Unofficial posters often appear, and candidates can send so-called private letters to their electors in sealed envelopes. It is even possible to launch a newspaper for a short period, for there is no maximum permitted expenditure in France. In metropolitan France, parties with candidates in at least 75 constituencies also have the right to a certain amount of radio and television time. In 1958, 12 parties qualified for this right.

Men and women may be both electors and candidates on exactly the same terms.

The most important innovation under the Fifth Republic is the requirement that all candidates, or all lists, where voting is by list,

[1] Civil servants and serving officers are disqualified from standing in constituencies in which they hold office or have held office within periods ranging in different cases, from six months to three years. An additional limitation was placed on candidates in Algeria in 1958; certain high officials and all soldiers having served in Algeria within the previous year were precluded from standing.

[2] In practice this means in the first ballot, except in the rare eventuality of a candidate dying between the two ballots, in which case his substitute replaces him at the second ballot.

must nominate a substitute[1] who will replace them if, after election, they die, or become disqualified from sitting owing to the new incompatibility rules—that is, if they accept Government office, or paid employment as an official of a trade union or other professional association, or appointment to the Constitutional Council, or membership of a Government mission lasting more than six months. In these cases, the substitute replaces the member until the following elections. If the member resigns, or becomes ineligible for any other reason, his seat is filled by a by-election.

The substitute is a 'shadow' Deputy. He is subject to the general rules governing candidature and must be qualified to vote. His name appears on the ballot paper along with that of the candidate, and the elector, in voting for the candidate, also votes contingently for his substitute. The substitute has certain privileges; for instance, he has none of the financial responsibilities for the campaign and is not obliged to take part in it, though he often did in 1958. He has also certain disabilities; if he does, in fact, replace the Deputy, he cannot oust him from his seat by standing against him at the following election. Deputies may not themselves act as substitutes for Senators, or *vice versa*,[2] nor may any substitute act for more than one Deputy.

In practice, in 1958, the substitute often tended to be used by the candidate as an adjunct in the electoral campaign—and one rather more useful than the candidate's wife usually is in England, since the candidate is free to choose his substitute at the time of the election. Candidates often did so in 1958, with the specific intention of attracting, or placating, certain sections of opinion, without involving themselves in any definite commitments to them.

Perhaps the best way to give some idea of the numbers and types

[1] In Algeria, lists include one European and one Moslem substitute. In the Oasis *département*, however, all three candidates are required to name a substitute.

[2] Those who drafted the electoral law had apparently not thought of this method, by which some Deputies and Senators could have ensured their membership of one House or the other, and a special Ordinance had to be promulgated forbidding its use.

E

of candidates contesting constituencies is to choose a few examples
In the *département* of the Eure, for instance, there were in the 195
elections, 24 candidates standing in four constituencies. They in
cluded 16 different political labels, and six distinct political ten
dencies (Communist, Socialist, Radical, Gaullist, Right, extrem
Right; there were no M.R.P. or U.D.S.R. candidates); seven of th
candidates were either Mayors of their *commune* or local Councillors
This is a typical *département*, since the average over the whol
country was six candidates per constituency. The lowest number o
candidates was two (in only one constituency), the highest 15. I
Paris, the third Sector (the Latin quarter) had 11 candidates repre
senting six political tendencies (Communist, Socialist, three Gaul
lists, three Right, extreme Right and the right-wing Catholi
movement, *Démocratie Chrétienne*; there were no Radical or M.R.P
candidates).

It is necessary to emphasize that this first election since 1936 hel
under the single-member system with two ballots was in many
respects unique in French history and that comparisons with th
results of previous elections under this system are not likely to b
very illuminating. It was held in an atmosphere of crisis in which th
dominant issue was that of confidence in General de Gaulle, a con
fidence expressed by the overwhelming majority of the candidates
many of whom were opposed to each other on everything else
General de Gaulle associated himself with no party and forbade hi
name to be used 'even as an adjective', but this rule was extensively
and ingeniously evaded. It was, indeed, often very difficult to
grasp from candidates' speeches or addresses what their policy was
Thus, to take one example, in St. Gaudens (Haute Garonne), th
candidate elected, an 80 year-old Radical, M. Hyppolite Ducos, who
had represented the region for 40 years, was one of six candidates
all of whom expressed themselves in favour of peace in Algeria
none of whom expressed themselves in favour of Algerian inde
pendence, and five of whom (that is excepting only the Communist
supported General de Gaulle.

It was also an election in which constituency boundaries were a new, and in which the system was also new to all electors under 40 and to two of the main parties, the U.N.R. and the M.R.P. There had been great population changes since 1936, and the Government, therefore, redrew boundaries on the basis of one representative per 93,000 inhabitants, and of a miniumum representation of two Deputies per *département*. In accordance with French tradition, constitutencies included, where possible, both rural and urban areas. These criteria resulted in the over-representation of the smaller *départements*, and also in some odd juxtapositions. Thus, for instance, the fashionable, and conservative, *commune* of Neuilly formed part of a constituency including the working-class, and Socialist, *commune* of Puteaux.

In the circumstances, accurate prediction of the results was impossible and they turned out to be a surprise for everybody, not least for the Ministry of the Interior. The Gaullists, who disliked the system, won a sweeping victory; Socialist Parliamentary strength was halved; Communist Parliamentary representation was almost wiped out; Radicals, who had been in favour of the system, fared badly; the M.R.P., which had always feared and disliked it, maintained its position.

There was, however, a striking disparity between the votes cast for the different parties and their Parliamentary representation, a disparity which resulted largely from political factors that had not been present at elections held under this system during the Third Republic. There was, first, the presence of some $2\frac{1}{2}$ million 'floating' votes, that had been cast for the Poujadist party in 1956; there was the presence of the M.R.P., a left-wing Catholic party, whose two million and more votes did not fit into the normal 'Left versus Right' pattern that had developed in pre-war elections under this system; there was an unbridgeable gulf between the two left-wing parties, Socialists and Communists, who, in the thirties, had been in the habit of combining against the Right at the second ballot; there were three Radical groups, where during the Third Republic there had been only one; and there was the totally unknown newcomer, the U.N.R., whose popularity was unknown and whose relations with the orthodox Right were confused and contradictory.

In theory, the single-member system is designed to strengthen moderate parties, since it puts at a disadvantage any party unable or unwilling to combine with others at the second ballot. In 1958 the Left *could* not combine, since Socialists and Communists had been in conflict since 1947; the Right in many cases *would* not. The result was that a larger number than usual of candidates maintained their candidature at the second ballot. In addition, either because parties or electors were not used to the discipline of the second ballot, or because the gravity of the circumstances was such that they considered it inapplicable, many of the electors ignored the recommendations of candidates who did stand down. Whatever they were advised to do, large numbers of electors belonging to all political tendencies (even including Communists) voted at the second ballot for the Gaullist candidate—that is, for the U.N.R., whose 'Gaullism' was its *raison d'être*.

It is clear that the electoral system could not in these circumstances have produced a representative Assembly. It produced what is probably the most unrepresentative Assembly in French history. Fifty Deputies represent the 7 million electors who voted for Socialist and Communist candidates while the 3½ million electors who voted for the U.N.R. are represented by over 200 Deputies. Whether this result will mean that, once again, there will be, if and when the opportunity occurs, a move to revise the electoral system, is a question that cannot as yet be answered.

(*b*) THE SENATE. In accordance with the practice of the two preceding régimes, the Senate is indirectly elected, mainly by local Councillors. It is, therefore, necessary to describe its electoral system in two stages; first the election of the electoral college itself, and second the system by which the Senators are elected.

In metropolitan France, Algeria, the Sahara,[1] and the four

---

[1] In Algeria, the constituency is not the *département*, but one or more of the 12 (effective) *départements* making a total of eight constituencies. In the two Saharan constituencies, the composition of the electoral college is slightly different.

Overseas *départements*, Senators are elected by a college consisting, in each *département*, of:

  (i) the Deputies representing the *département*,
  (ii) the Councillors representing the *département*,
  (iii) Municipal Councillors, whose number varies according to the population;
   (*a*) *Communes* with populations of 9,000–30,000, and the 60 *Communes* of the Seine, irrespective of their population, are represented by all Municipal Councillors.
   (*b*) *Communes* with populations of over 30,000 have, in addition the right to an additional delegate for every 1,000 inhabitants over 30,000.
   (*c*) *Communes* with populations of under 9,000 (that is 37,518 of the 38,000 *communes*) choose from among their Municipal Councillors from 1–15 delegates, according to their population.

In the five Overseas Territories, each of which elects one Senator, the electoral college is similarly composed, except that special arrangements have to be made for representatives of *communes* that do not yet have fully elective Councils.

Four different systems are employed in the election of the 307 Senators.

  (i) In *départements* represented by one to four Senators, that is, in all but seven of the 90 *départments* of France, in the four Overseas *départements* and the five Overseas Territories, election is by the majority system, with two ballots. To be elected at the first ballot, candidates must obtain an absolute majority of the votes cast and a number of votes equal to at least a quarter of the electorate. At the second ballot a relative majority only is required. 209 Senators (195 metropolitan Senators, seven for the Overseas *départements*, two for the Sahara and five for the Overseas Territories) are elected on this system.
  (ii) In the seven heavily populated *départements* of France[1] which

[1] These are: Nord, Pas-de-Calais, Rhône, Seine, Seine Maritime, Seine-et-Oise and Bouches-du-Rhône.

have five or more Senators, election is by proportional representation (the highest average system). Sixty metropolitan Senators are elected in this way.

(iii) In the eight Algerian constituencies, electing 32 Senators, the system is also that of the majority system with two ballots, but voting is for lists on which European and Moslem candidates are represented in fixed proportions; ten represent the European and 22 the Moslem communities. Any list obtaining an absolute majority of the votes at the first ballot is declared elected. A relative majority only is required at the second.

(iv) The six Senators representing French residents abroad are chosen in the first instance by the High Council of French residents abroad, composed of *ex-officio* and elected members and of members nominated by the Ministry of Foreign Affairs, from names submitted by its different regional sections. The Council's choice must be ratified by the Senate. If 30 Senators oppose any nomination, a secret ballot takes place on all. A relative majority only is required for election.

Senators are elected for nine years, a third retiring every three years.[1] Candidates must be aged at least 35. Other qualifications are the same as those required for election to the Assembly, including the obligation to name a substitute.[2]

This system is criticized for the same reasons as were those governing elections to the Second Chamber of both the Third and Fourth Republics. The fact that election is for nine years (six under the Fourth Republic) and that the electors themselves may

[1] Exceptionally, in 1959, all Senators were elected at the same time. The 307 are divided into three 'series', A, B, and C, each including a third of the Senators. It was decided by lot that series A should be renewed in 1962, series B in 1965 and series C in 1968.

[2] In *départements* where election is by proportional representation, the candidate coming next on the list following the last elected candidate acts as the substitute. All substitutes called on to replace Senators hold office only until the following partial renewal. A by-election is then held to fill seats which would not normally be filled at that time.

have been elected from four to six years earlier means that there is a danger of Senators being out of touch with public opinion. The electoral college over-represents small rural areas. Over half of the Senatorial electors represent villages with fewer than 1,500 inhabitants. Towns with populations of 10,000 and upwards are represented by only just over a fifth of the Senatorial electors, though they constitute over 40 per cent of the population. The provision that every *département*, however small, has at least one Senator, and the general over-representation of the smaller *départements*, help to increase the unbalance. Thus, the *département* of the Lot, with a population of 147,000, has one Senator. Those of Basses Alpes and Hautes Alpes, with populations of between 80–90,000, each have one Senator. At the other end of the scale, the Seine *département*, with a population of almost five millions, has 22 and the Nord, with a population of two millions, has 9—one for every quarter of a million.

In essence, this is the system by which the Council of the Republic was elected under the previous régime.[1] It is, therefore, not surprising that the first elections to the Senate of the Fifth Republic should have resulted in the election of a high percentage of personalities of the Fourth. Eighty-four per cent of the retiring Senators who presented themselves for re-election were returned. And among the 85 new Senators, 35 were former Members of Parliament; 29 were Deputies who had lost their seats in the elections of November 1958 including party leaders such as MM. Edgar Faure, Mitterrand, Deferre, Duclos, Bonnefous. It has been suggested that the Senate, with its increased complement of practised Parliamentary performers, might, at least during the first Parliament of the Fifth Republic, attract more public interest than the Assembly.

---

[1] The main changes are the reduction of the number of *départments* in which election is by proportional representation from 11 to seven (from those with four Senators to those with five or more), and the slight increase in the representation of large towns. Electoral colleges under the Fourth Republic included additional delegates only for towns of over 45,000 inhabitants, and only one delegate for every 5,000 inhabitants over that figure.

CHAPTER V

Parties

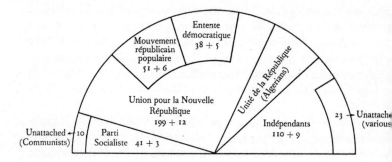

Groups in the National Assembly as on 22nd October 1959.
+ sign indicates affiliates.

Permanent characteristics of the French party system

The French party system has a number of permanent characteristics, some of which appear inconsistent with each other. The first is the multiplicity of parties. In a general election, what could be called 'national' parties number anything from 12 to 20, and there are also a varying number of less important formations, some local, some ephemeral, some consisting of little more than a label attached to some personality or special interest. Between nine and 15 groups are normally represented in the Assembly, some of them with smaller affiliated groups, and some with closely related organizations outside the Assembly.

There is also a great diversity in both their organization and their politics. They cover a range extending from Communism on the Left to anti-Parliamentary and even Fascist groups on the extreme Right. Some attach great importance to political principles and doctrines and will expel members who stray openly or continuously from the orthodox path. Others appear to have no general principles and some have no coherent policy. Radicalism, for instance, has been described as a state of mind, while French conservatism is, more than anything else, a collection of special interests, often in conflict with each other. Party organization varies from the organized and disciplined parties on the Left, whose policy is formulated at party congresses attended by delegates representing local federations, and in meetings of the Parliamentary group, to the constantly changing right-wing parties, some of which have no permanent organization outside the Assembly, and whose Parliamentary groups are regularly divided. In between is the Radical party, which does have an extra-Parliamentary organization and discusses policy at party congresses, but which has never had either a large mass membership or a disciplined group in the Assembly. When M. Mendès-France was leader of the party, he tried to turn it into an organized and disciplined party. In 1957, it was decided that, once the Parliamentary group had taken a decision, members must respect it; they were entitled to abstain, but not to vote against. A fortnight later, the group decided to vote for M. Mollet, who was then trying to form a Government. In the event, 21 voted for, eight abstained and 13 voted against. This is an average sample of a Radical vote in the Assembly.

There is no French party in any way comparable with any of the three British parties. Until the '50's there was no large conservative party. There were extra-Parliamentary organizations, such as the pre-war *Fédération Républicaine*, and a number of independent and shifting Parliamentary groups. Even now, the *Centre National des Indépendants*, which includes the bulk of the Parliamentary conservatives, is not a party, but a federation loosely held together. It is not responsible for policy, and has no unified organization in the country.

Nor has there ever been in France any political formation

remotely resembling the British Liberal party. France has Radical parties and parties of social reform; many of her parties are internationalist and individualist; but the special combination of Radicalism, free-trade, international idealism and social reformism, Protestantism, individualism and love of liberty that goes to make up Liberalism has never been found in a single party, and some of the elements—Protestantism and free-trade, for instance—are virtually non-existent.

The French Socialist party has a divided inheritance, in which the reformist and humanitarian idealism of Jaurès is allied to the doctrinaire and theoretical approach of Guesde, and the pluralist and syndicalist views of Proudhon exist alongside, but mix ill with, the 'scientific' Socialism of Marx. Though it uses the vocabulary of a class party and pays lip service to the concept of the class war, its members include a high proportion of middle-class intellectuals—teachers, and civil servants in particular—and of black-coated workers. It suffers, as does the predominantly Catholic M.R.P. from the organizational divorce between political parties and trade unions which exists in France.

Another characteristic of French parties is their fluidity. Parties come and go in bewildering numbers, sometimes within a very short time, It was pointed out in the last chapter that the six elections since the war had seen the spectacular rise of four new, major parties, and the equally rapid disappearance of two of them. A glance at the list of political groups in the Assembly, over the same period of time, would show that well over 20 new Parliamentary formations made their appearance, of which 15 or more disappeared after one or two sessions. Many of these never had any existence outside the Assembly, but at least half-a-dozen did, and others were formed in the country but were never represented in Parliament.

Yet, as has also been pointed out in earlier chapters, one of the most striking characteristics of French politics is the stability of political tendencies. Since the war, three electors in four have voted regularly for one of six tendencies, of which three—Conservative, Radical and Socialist—go back over half a century, and the fourth,

Communist, over a quarter of a century. Of the other two, the progressive Catholic M.R.P. has existed since the war, and some small pre-war groups also represented a similar point of view. Only Gaullism is a wholly post-war product, and that, too, includes elements whose inheritance goes some way back in history.

The combination of stability of opinion and instability of political organizations has no single or simple explanation. Parties are divided, partly owing to the highly developed individualism of the French character, partly owing to the relatively more important rôle played by personalities in French politics than in systems like the British. Divisions are encouraged by the interplay of economic interests on the Right and doctrinal conflicts on the Left. The divisions lead to splits and splinter groups, instead of subsisting as tendencies within a party, partly because the existence of a multi-party system tends, in itself, to remove the electoral incentives to unity that characterize a two-party system like the British; partly because France's economic stability enabled her, up to the second world war, to indulge in the luxury of political and party squabbles that a more economically vulnerable country could not afford; partly, too, because of the greater number of issues on which divisions were bitter and intransigent, and because of the length of French political memories.

The impermanence of party alignments under the Fifth Republic

From time to time in French history, the permanent tendencies just described have been jolted out of their familiar ruts by a national crisis or controversy, which, for a time, has either split the country in two, as the Dreyfus affair did, or as the division between resisters and collaborators did during the war, or which has dominated political thinking to the exclusion of almost anything else, as the controversy on German rearmament did between 1952 and 1954. Since French political memories are long, some of these controversies survive as political issues long after the original problem has become part of history, as the anti-clerical issue has done.

The events of 13th May 1958 were caused by a crisis and in turn provoked a controversy of the kind just described. For the time being, the attitudes of French parties are dominated by their approach to the three interrelated problems of Algeria, General de Gaulle's rôle in the State, and the provisions of the new Constitution. The result of the apparent insolubility of the Algerian problem, and of its relation to the other two, has been that new parties have appeared seeking some new approach, and that old parties are divided within themselves or have actually split on these issues. Almost all French parties today, except the Communists, have break-away, or minority sections, whose differences from the majority of the party are due entirely to the present crisis, and whose separation may not, therefore, be permanent. The 'autonomous' Socialists are opposed to the new régime, to its Algerian policy and to the personality of M. Guy Mollet, who is associated in their minds with both. M. Bidault's *Démocratie Chrétienne* is opposed to the M.R.P.'s Algerian and foreign policies. The U.D.S.R. has split into a pro- and an anti-Gaullist section. The Mendésiste Radicals disagree with the *Valoisien* party mainly on this problem, though there are also both personal and political points of friction. Most of the 71 Deputies for Algeria have no policy on any issue except that of Algeria.

Since the normal business of government has to be carried on, parties are inevitably obliged to take stands on other problems in the course of a Parliamentary session. But the first sessions of the Fifth Republic were naturally occupied for some time in setting up the new organs provided for in the Constitution and in drafting the Parliamentary Standing Orders. The legislative programmes were slight and, on the whole, relatively non-controversial. The budgetary debates revealed the familiar divisions on economic and financial policy. While the Algerian problem dominates everything else, the situation is bound to remain abnormal and unstable and parties are, to a much greater extent than usual, unorientated, seeking new orientations, or, when they fail to find them, either biding their time in the hope of being able to go back to old orientations, or frankly falling back on traditional behaviour. Familiarity is, after all, a common substitute for security.

The static Right

The last-mentioned attitude is, comprehensibly, the predominating characteristic of the orthodox right-wing parties. It will be clear from what has already been said that there is no such thing as a Conservative policy. But there are Conservative attitudes. •In economic affairs, the French Right is opposed to State control of industry and to State intervention in the interests of a planned economy, but in favour of State action to assist producers, often small and uneconomic producers.•Right-wing Deputies regularly support price-fixing in the interests of small farmers, subsidies to the wine-growers of the south and to the beetroot producers of the north, and fiscal privileges to agricultural producers and to the three million or more home distillers.• In social matters, the right-wing groups defend Catholic claims to State aid for Catholic schools. In the political field, they favour a nationalist foreign policy (*la politique de la grandeur*) though, when it comes to budget debates, they are usually unwilling to foot the bills and call for economies in State expenditure.•They are opposed to what they term 'abandonment' of French possessions overseas and have always accepted with the greatest reluctance any move towards limited home rule in Algeria and the Overseas Territories. They support the policy of integration, summarized by the slogan *Algérie française*. Of recent years, a small right-wing anti-colonialist tendency has developed, arguing (with truth) that the French overseas possessions are a financial liability. This tendency is small and, at present, wholly without influence.

In general, orthodox right-wing parties support General de Gaulle's leadership, though there is little love lost between the *indépendents* (the main Conservative group in the Assembly) and the Gaullists. Among older right-wing Parliamentarians there is active dislike of the diminished rôle of Parliament in the Fifth Republic, little sympathy for Gaullist ideas of 'renewal' and even less for the fiscal reforms and increased taxes which the new régime has introduced.

The extreme Right

Small, extremist, right-wing groups, whose numbers and influence fluctuate according to the political situation, have always been a feature of French political life. Groups such as *Jeune Nation, le Front National Français, Réconciliation Française, le Parti Nationaliste*, and *le Mouvement du 13 Mai* have all been in existence some time during the Fifth Republic. Little is known of the membership figures of those that exist in more than name, but they are certainly small. The influence of such groups is normally negligible but they could become important in the event of some new 13 May, which they would enthusiastically support, as some of them supported the last. They agree in opposing the liberal elements of General de Gaulle's policy, their general attitude being that of the Algerian 'ultras'.

This is also the position of what remains of M. Poujade's movement. Most of the two and a half millions who voted for Poujadist candidates in 1956 seem to have supported orthodox right-wing candidates in 1958. The movement is now small, disunited and has no representation in Parliament, though it is in sympathy with (if not allied to) the Peasant group in the Assembly, which is on the right of the *Indépendants*. It no longer has any real influence in the country.

Some 50 of the 71 Deputies representing Algeria also represent the 'ultra' point of view. Now known as the 'Group for the Unity of the Republic', they really constitute a pressure group rather than a party, since their predominant interest is Algeria and they have no policy on any other issue. And even on the policy of 'integration' there are disagreements among them. Up to July 1959, they remained what was called 'an administrative formation', that is they were allowed temporarily to be represented on Commissions as if they constituted an organized group, without having made a declaration of policy. They have now regularized their situation but their declaration consisted of a six-point programme, of which five points related to Algeria, the sixth expressing their support for 'a general policy of greatness and national independence'.

Some of the Moslem members for Algeria, and a handful of Europeans, with a more liberal point of view, have joined other groups.

The dynamic Right. Is Gaullism conservative?

The specific form of dynamism called Gaullism does not lend itself
to precise definition. To begin with, the Gaullists, either in the
Assembly or outside, do not really constitute a party at all, in the
accepted sense of the term. The Gaullist organization is united
only on two things. Its members accept the leadership of General
de Gaulle and they believe in the need for a national 'renewal' (*le
renouveau français*). General de Gaulle, however, has consistently
refused to be associated with any party (though his refusal to allow
the movement to describe itself as Gaullist applied only to the period
of the electoral campaign), and the leaders of the party are agreed
neither on the rôle that they want him to play, nor on the methods
by which French renewal is to be achieved. For six years, during
the Fourth Republic, the Gaullist Rally of the French People had both
a leader and a programme. But the movement was disbanded in
1955, General de Gaulle's association with it being officially severed.
His association with Gaullist members of Parliament had already
been severed two years earlier. Gaullism under the Fifth Republic
had so far neither united leadership, nor a programme.

Gaullism includes at least half a dozen tendencies. The so-called
Gaullist party, the Union for the New Republic (U.N.R.) was
formed only a few weeks before the 1958 election, by the fusion of
four Gaullist movements of very different political complexions.
The Social Republicans constituted the sole remnant of the pre-war
Gaullist organization, represented in the 1956 Assembly by some
20 Deputies. The Union for French Renewal (*Union pour le Renouveau Français*) was founded by M. Soustelle, himself a Social
Republican Deputy, as an extension into France of an Algerian
movement representing the settler point of view. M. Soustelle, a
former Governor-General of Algeria, was very popular with the
European population of that country. He is a firm believer in the
policy of '*Algérie française*'. His part in the revolution of 13th

May was to maintain enthusiasm for the policy of 'integration'
following the demonstrations of Franco-Moslem fraternization from
16th May onwards, and he made a number of speeches on this subject
at the time, both in Algiers and elsewhere. He is an able politician
and a talented orator. Since the formation of the first Government
of the Fifth Republic, in which he holds a high position, he has made
only the most guarded and vague statements about integration.

The other two constituent groups of the U.N.R. were the Repub
lican Convention, led by M. Delbecque, who also played an active
rôle in the events (and even more in the preparation) of 13th May
and the Workers' Committee for the support of General de Gaulle
Both were formed to support General de Gaulle in the campaign for
the referendum.[1]

Once the election of 1958 was over, the Parliamentary group of
over 200 Deputies belonging to the U.N.R. had to work out a
policy. It found itself divided on questions of leadership and
organization, as well as on questions of policy. When the party's
first Secretary-General, M. Frey, became a Minister, he was succeeded temporarily by M. Chalandon, a liberal economist, who
believes in economic expansion, a progressive social policy and a
'liberal' solution for Algeria. The U.N.R. is, in his mind, a dynamic, but not a conservative party.

M. Chalandon's approach was that of a technocrat, for whom the
party ought to consist of *cadres*, whose function should be to carry
out faithfully the policies of General de Gaulle. Both on policy and
on organization he found himself in conflict with the tendency
represented by M. Soustelle and M. Delbecque, who believed that
the party's electoral popularity had depended almost entirely on
its association in the minds of the electors with General de Gaulle
and that what was needed was its transformation into a mass party
with a modern organization.

[1] A great many so-called Gaullist organizations, most of them short-lived
were set up both in Algeria and in France from 13th May onwards. They
ranged from Fascist and near-Fascist 'activist' formations implicated in the
insurrection to relatively left-wing organizations.

The future of Gaullism must remain for some time full of uncertainties. The rank and file of the U.N.R. include some near-
Fascist elements—some U.N.R. Deputies have been described as
'more 13th May than Gaullist'. Developments in the Algerian
situation, or in the relations between army and State, could bring
these authoritarian tendencies to the top. At the other extreme,
outside the ranks of the U.N.R., there are the left-wing Gaullists,
divided between the *Centre de la Réforme Républicaine* and the *Union
Démocratique du Travail*, movements which are numerically small and
include a number of intellectuals, but which are not far removed
politically from the more progressive elements inside the U.N.R.

Gaullism, then, could develop in a number of different ways. It
could become a new authoritarian Right, or a new centre party,
replacing the old Radical party as an essential element of Governmental majorities. It could remain a heterogeneous movement, acting
as would-be agent of General de Gaulle, rather than an independent
party, or it could split up into several independent groups, as the pre-
war R.P.F. did, and consequently cease either to ensure a Governmental majority in the Assembly or to exert any real ininfluence in
the country. It could disappear as rapidly as it appeared, owing either
to the fickleness of the electorate or to the disappearance from the
political scene, for whatever reason, of General de Gaulle himself.[1]

The policy of Gaullism is inseparable from the problem of its
future. While the different tendencies have been fighting out their
battles within the party, official declarations of the party's attitude

[1] M. Chalandon has expressed views consistent with both the conception
of the party as an agent for General de Gaulle and that of a centre party. Cf.,
for instance, 'General de Gaulle is our clandestine leader. We are rather like
secret agents, owing total obedience to their military leader, who will not hesitate to disavow them if things go badly' (quoted in *Le Monde*, 21st July 1959),
and the following extract from an article in the Gaullist press bulletin: 'We are
a party movement and, consequently, the negation of traditional conservatism.
. . We are also a liberal party. . . . We have strengthened the power of the
executive, but in order to safeguard essential liberties. . . . Lastly, we are a
Governmental party. . . . We are bound to support Governments, of whatever kind, to be the pivot of majorities; they will be perhaps Left, perhaps

F

have been either apologia for the Government, or compromise statements of great generality and little meaning. In the Assembly, the group at first voted as a disciplined unit, though not without some friction between personalities and tendencies. Indeed, the need for discipline in the party appeared to be one of its few agreed and firmly held convictions.

The static Left. Has Radicalism a future?

The Radical party is the oldest French party, but its influence has been declining since the '30's, when the Socialist party became a serious rival in the traditional Radical strongholds. It almost disappeared during the early post-war years, though, by 1955, had recovered to the extent of having some 75 Deputies in the Assembly (including associates and the U.D.S.R.), and of having provided eight of the 16 Prime Ministers who had held office since the beginning of the Fourth Republic. From 1955 onwards, it was weakened by three successive splits. M. Faure's *Rassemblement des Gauches Républicaines* (R.G.R.) was an electoral coalition, re-formed as a party after his expulsion from the Radical party, along with several others, following the 1955 dissolution. The R.G.R.'s differences from the parent party were personal rather than political. In 1956, a dissident group was formed, consisting of a dozen or so of the more right-wing representatives in the Assembly, including two former Prime Ministers, MM. Marie and Queuille. This group differed mainly from the orthodox Radicals on Algerian policy, being in favour of '*l'Algérie française*'.[1] In 1958, M. Mendès-France and a handful of his supporters on the left of the party were deemed to have excluded themselves, owing to their refusal to resign, on the in-

Right, but, in any case, we shall be there.' (Quoted in *Le Monde*, 19th May 1959.)

On the policy of Gaullism under the Fourth Republic, *v*. Philip Williams, *Politics in post-war France* (Longmans, 1954) and, for a brief discussion, the author's *France: The Fourth Republic* (Methuen, 1958).

[1] This group was usually called the *Centre Républicain*, though in 1958, it announced its title as being *Le Parti de la Gauche Démocratique et Radical socialiste*.

structions of the party, from the left-wing electoral alliance the *Union des Forces Démocratiques*. The Radicals (all tendencies) lost about half a million votes in the 1958 elections. The *Entente Démocratique* group in the Assembly, in 1959, is made up of orthodox Radicals, now calling themselves *La Gauche Démocratique et Radical-socialiste*, and a formation calling itself *Libertés Démocratiques*, which includes some former members of the U.D.S.R., of the Radical party and of the *Centre Républicain*.

Since the war, Radicalism has been, in economic policy, conservative, though M. Mendès-France tried between 1955 and 1957, when he was acting chairman of the party, to give it a modern organization and a more left-wing economic policy. Both attempts failed. It remains, as it has always been, politically on the Left, strongly Republican, believing in democratic Parliamentary government, and anti-clerical, though somewhat less fervently so than it used to be.[1]

On Algeria, the party's policy is progressive, the majority insisting both on the need to recognize the 'Algerian personality', and on the irrelevance of independence to Algeria's special problems. The majority of the party has been in favour of negotiations for a cease-fire, followed by negotiations with representative Algerians on a future status for Algeria. The party has supported General de Gaulle, though with misgivings regarding the Government's economic policy and the Constitution's failure to provide for effective Parliamentary supervision of the Government.

The Catholic Left

In matters of social and economic policy, the M.R.P. (*Mouvement*

[1] A party politically close to the Radicals is the U.D.S.R. (*Union Démocratique et Socialiste de la Résistance*) which was, as its name implies, a post-war formation, arising out of a war-time resistance movement. Politically, it is somewhat to the Left of the majority of the Radicals. It has never been strong outside Parliament, and has had to rely on alliances with other small groups, often including a high proportion of overseas Deputies, in order to qualify as a recognized Parliamentary group. It has been important mainly because it has included leading personalities, such as MM. Pleven, Mitterand and Claudius-Petit. The events of 13th May and the return of General de Gaulle led to a split, M. Pleven being pro- and M. Mitterand anti-Gaullist.

Républicain Populaire) is definitely farther to the Left than the Radicals (except for those in sympathy with M. Mendès-France). But, though it is firmly Republican and democratic, the movement has found it difficult to establish itself as an authentic left-wing party, for several reasons. It has existed only since the war and has not yet managed to get a firm hold in the traditionally-minded country areas except in the predominantly Catholic *départements* of Eastern and Western France. Though by no means all its members are Catholics, it is strongly influenced by Catholicism, as are the numerous Youth and Women's organizations associated with it. And on the question that is almost a test of left-wing *bona fides*, the Catholic schools problem, the M.R.P. shares the views of the Right. It has often been supported by electors who are more conservative than the majority of its leaders. As a predominantly Catholic, anti-Marxist, anti-class-war party, preaching the virtues of family life, a party whose loyalty to General de Gaulle in the early post-war period gained for it the description of *le parti de la fidélité*, the M.R.P. has been, from a right-wing point of view, a respectable substitute if, for any reason, right-wing candidates were unacceptable in a constituency. For the same reasons, the M.R.P. tended to be unacceptable to the Socialists. The battle over the *loi Barangé*, which, in 1951, provided a small State contribution to Catholic schools, led to the alienation of the M.R.P. and Socialist parties from each other throughout the second Parliament of the Fourth Republic.

The success, in the 1956 elections, of a number of younger candidates, whose views reflected those of the strong Catholic Trade Union Confederation, the C.F.T.C. (*Confédération des Travailleurs Chrétiens*) and the removal of some of the more right-wing elements from the party with the formation of M. Bidault's *Démocratie Chrétienne*[1] after the events of 13th May, helped to strengthen the leftward orientation of the party. Its internal organization, which

---

[1] *Démocratie Chrétienne* has been 'integrationist', in favour of *Algérie française*, of a strong French foreign policy in general and of French firmness in the intermittent and apparently endless negotiations on Franco-Tunisian relations.

is democratic, was modified, from 1958 onwards, in order to give to rank and file members, and especially workers and peasants, half the places in the executive organs of the party.

The M.R.P.'s policy in relation to Algeria has, at times, appeared to be more progressive than that of the Socialist party. The movement has favoured a negotiated settlement, but has had confidence in General de Gaulle's intentions regarding Algeria. It also favours a policy of aid to under-developed areas, often advocated by General de Gaulle in his speeches up and down the country. In foreign affairs, it is the only party to have been consistently and unanimously in favour of the policy of European integration and has been, more than any other section of opinion, responsible for France's moves in that direction. In internal affairs it believes in a policy of economic expansion and deplores the social inequalities resulting from the Government's economic policy. It is also suspicious of the technocratic tendencies of the Fifth Republic.

Socialism and 'constructive opposition'

After a brief post-war period of great prestige and influence, the Socialist party lost votes steadily until about 1955, from which point, up to the end of the Fourth Republic, it began to gain ground, though, in 1958, its membership figures were still not more than half those of 1946. The composition of the party was, moreover, increasingly middle-class and middle-aged.

The party had to face great practical difficulties throughout the Fourth Republic. With the passage of the Communist party into opposition in 1947, it had to compete for working-class votes with a party which could, and did, exploit to the full the opportunities for political irresponsibility offered by opposition, while the Socialist party was often compelled either to support, or to participate in Governments, the majority of whose members were considerably to its right. Socialist party organization was ill-adapted to the needs of a party in office, being traditionally organized to give full expression to all tendencies within the party. M. Guy Mollet, who became Secretary-General in 1946, was largely responsible for making the party a disciplined organ of decision, but incurred great unpopularity with the numerically small but influential minority, which had been opposed to the majority view on German rearmament, on Algeria, on General de Gaulle's return to power and on the Constitution.

The Socialist party's Algerian policy consisted of a three-point programme (known in the movement as the 'triptych') aiming at military pacification, free elections and negotiations. In essence, this is the programme that most liberal opinion, including the Socialists, has considered to be General de Gaulle's policy, with the difference that General de Gaulle decided to hold elections, in spite of the continuance of the fighting. Under the Fifth Republic, the party continued to advocate negotiations for a cease-fire and, either consequently or simultaneously, efforts to negotiate a settlement. There have been differences of emphasis, even within the majority, and also between the majority and the minority.

In September 1958, the minority broke away and formed an independent party, its candidates opposing those of the parent party in the elections. All the candidates of the 'autonomous' party were defeated. Ideologically, there is no real difference of opinion between majority and minority. Both remain faithful to anti-clericalism to the (partially) Marxist inheritance, these sentiments being particularly strong among the rank and file. On the problems confronting the Fifth Republic in its early years, the differences have been important. The majority party's position has been one of 'constructive opposition', by which was meant co-operation as far as possible with General de Gaulle in his efforts to save the Republic and to bring peace to Algeria, but opposition to specific aspects of the Government's policy, especially to its economic restrictionism and its fiscal and social policies, which, the party believed, placed too big a burden on the working class. In foreign policy, the party has remained faithful to the policy of European integration, though being generally less united on it, and less interested in it, than the M.R.P. It is firmly opposed to any association, either electoral or on specific issues, with the Communist party.

On this last point the 'autonomous' minority has taken up a

much less firm position. It has tried to unite a number of small parties or movements that are in opposition to the régime, some of which include fellow-travellers, ex-Communists and members of predominantly intellectual left-wing groups, such as the *Union de la Gauche Socialiste*. Its members are in sympathy with, and some are members of, the left-wing movement, the *Union des Forces Démocratiques*, formed during the 1958 crisis in support of the Fourth Republic. There are doctrinal differences within the autonomous movement and it seems to combine nostalgia for the past, in matters of internal policy, with a somewhat neutralist attitude in foreign policy. In September 1959, the Mendésiste Radical group, the *Centre d'Action Démocratique*, joined the autonomous Socialist party.

The Communist Party

Except for a few months in 1946, the Communist party has consistently polled more votes than any other party. Even in the 1958 elections, which resulted in the reduction of its Parliamentary representation from 142 to ten Deputies, the party polled 3,882,204 votes at the first ballot. This total showed a drop of over a million and a half on the 1956 figures, but it was still over 200,000 higher than the total of the votes cast for the Gaullist U.N.R.

The strength of Communism in a country like France, with a high proportion of craftsmen and small owner-farmers, and with a highly individualist and critical approach to politics, is perhaps, at first sight, surprising. In the context of left-wing Republican and Revolutionary tradition it is less so. Part of the Communist party's strength comes from its claim to be, at the same time, Republican and Revolutionary, whole-heartedly Marxist and the most left-wing party. Its position of permanent opposition, since 1947, has given it ample opportunity to demonstrate its interest in the workers. Its closely-knit internal organization, based on occupational 'cells' more than on local branches, and its real (though not, of course, admitted) control of the oldest and strongest of the trade union organizations, the C.G.T. (*Confédération Générale du Travail*) have given it an efficient organization, able to back up its demands, by strike action if necessary.

Communism also has a strong ideological attraction for left-wing intellectuals, whose influence is strong in France in the numerous left-wing literary and political periodicals which are concerned with Communist doctrine as well as with current political problems. This element contributes to the spread of Communist propaganda, but at times has also constituted a weakness. The fact that some intellectuals insist on thinking for themselves has involved, of recent years, a number of tortuous doctrinal controversies and one or two spectacular departures from the party. And the events in Hungary, on which a number of Communist intellectuals openly attacked the orthodox point of view and some resigned from the party, dealt the Communists the most severe blow that they had received since the outbreak of war in 1939.

The Communist party reacted to the events of 13th May, first, by calling for demonstrations of loyalty to the Republic, especially for strikes, and then by declaring its opposition to the new régime. Both the response to Communist appeals and the voting figures in the referendum and elections revealed, however, that whether for political reasons (the persistence of the feeling regarding Hungary, or the unpopularity of its support for the Algerian rebels) or for economic reasons (the unpopularity of political strikes) the party had lost much of its former hold over its supporters.[1] In the referendum, only four and a half million electors voted *No*, whereas in 1956, five and a half million electors had voted for the Communist party. The result was that, for the first year or so of the new régime, apart from one abortive strike threat which was not of purely Communist inspiration, the Communist party remained very much in the background, advocating united working-class action. This has almost always been a sign of Communist consciousness of weakness. In Parliament, the party had no longer any influence, since its small numbers deprived it of both representation on Commissions and

[1] There has been a sharp drop in the number and sales of Communist papers, particularly in the provinces. This may be partly due to the sudden fall in Communist income owing to the reduction in the number of Communist Party Deputies, all of whom contribute a considerable share of their income to the party.

the possibility of introducing motions of censure. The Assembly also consistently refused to nominate Communists to other bodies, such as the Senate of the Community. The danger was, therefore, that the party would concentrate its attention on the industrial field, where it still had considerable influence, and might soon have more if the Government's economic policy seriously affected the standard of living for the working class.

Public opinion

The state of public opinion in the first year of the Fifth Republic seemed no less apathetic than it had been during the last weeks of the Fourth Republic. The traditional parties were still tending to look backwards, while the one forward-looking party, the U.N.R., had still no clear concept of where it was trying to go. The situation produced by the *coup* of 13th May was one that all parties were ill-adapted to meet. It was a revolutionary situation, but the threat of revolution was of a new kind. The army in Algeria constitutes, in the Fifth Republic, a kind of fourth Estate, about whose attitude very little reliable information is available. With the exception of the Communist party, however, the French Left has begun to realize that the kind of revolution with which it threatened France would not be affected by marches from the *Place de la Nation* to the *Place de la République*, or *vice versa*, nor even by resistance on the barricades. It has also become increasingly aware of the fact that the public could still not be counted on to man any barricades. For this state of affairs, the Fourth Republic's achievements, as well as its failures, were responsible. Its great achievement was an economic recovery, which had created general prosperity, and a real rise in the standard of living of the working class. Its failures were its political divisions, and the constant Governmental deadlocks, together with the inability of successive Governments to solve a certain number of vital problems, which had led to political apathy. The Communist party's share of responsibility in these failures is enormous. It is more difficult to decide where the responsibility lies for the continued strength and influence of the Communist party.

CHAPTER VI

Parliament

The Constitution deals with legislative procedure in much more detail than previous Constitutions have done. A number of matters traditionally left for Parliament to decide are now constitutionalized. Parliamentary Standing Orders, for instance, must now be submitted to the Constitutional Council and declared in conformity with the Constitution, before they can come into force; Governments are specifically given control over matters previously controlled by Parliament. The Assembly's Standing Orders, too, have themselves prohibited devices much used by previous Assemblies (and also by the Senate) in order to harass and weaken Governments,[1] and have provided for a greater measure of control by the President of the Assembly, in order to prevent the indiscipline and disorder that have sometimes characterized debates in the Assembly. The result is, on paper, an Assembly diminished in power, in relation to the Government, and in prestige in relation to the Senate. Whether the theory will be effectively translated into practice will depend, in the first instance, on the way in which members of Parliament use the considerable rights that they still possess, which is the subject of this chapter, and, in the second instance, on the relations that are established, in practice, between Government and Assembly, which will be discussed in the following chapter.

The Rights and Duties of Members of Parliament

Members of Parliament enjoy certain privileges. In order that they may speak and vote freely, they are not liable, either during or

[1] *v.* below, pp. 119–26.

after their membership of either House, to criminal or civil proceedings in respect of anything said or done by them in the House in the exercise of their duties. They remain responsible for anything said or published outside Parliament. While Parliament is sitting, proceedings may not be taken against them for anything said or done in their private capacity, unless the House of which they are members decides, by a vote, to suspend their immunity. Exceptions to the rule are minor offences, the penalty for which would not prevent them from carrying out their Parliamentary duties, and serious offences, in which the member is caught *flagrante delicto*. In the latter case, he may be arrested, though the House is still free to stop proceedings. When Parliament is not sitting proceedings are possible but, except in cases where the arrest is *flagrante delicto*, or where a Court has made a final finding of guilt, or where arrest has been authorized in a previous session, the member may be arrested only with the authorization of the *bureau* of the House.

Members are also subject to certain obligations. Certain occupations are incompatible with membership of Parliament. Those which entail the member's replacement by a substitute have been mentioned in the previous chapter.[1] In the case of other incompatibilities, the member's resignation is followed by a by-election. Most of the incompatibilities existed also under the Third and Fourth Republics. They include directorships of nationalized and State-subsidized concerns, or of concerns carrying out public-works contracts. The Fifth Republic has added to the list that of the legal representation of concerns involved in actions against the State. Membership in an unpaid capacity of local Government authorities and of certain local non-profit-making concerns are specifically excepted from the list of incompatibilities.[2]

[1] *v. supra*, pp. 65–6.
[2] Three traditional exceptions are also holders of university chairs (and now also of research chairs), members of Government missions (of under six months' duration) and ministers of religion in the three *départements* of Alsace-Lorraine, still governed in religious matters by the *Concordat*.

Mandatory instructions to members of Parliament (*le mandat impératif*) are null and void. The interpretation of this rule (article 27 of the Constitution) has given rise to some discussion, since Deputies and Senators who belong to an organized party clearly do vote in accordance with a mandate from their parties, and also with decisions of their Parliamentary group. It is generally accepted that the intention of this article is to prohibit, not the normal working of democratic party machinery, but the kind of party domination represented by the Communist party's habit of requiring Communist members to place a signed resignation form in the hands of the party, to be used as the party, and not the member, sees fit. In other words, the member is intended to be, as Burke maintained he was, a national representative and not merely a delegate of special interests.

It is difficult, nevertheless, to see any practical utility in this prohibition, since, except in the case of a flagrant and generally known practice such as that quoted above, proof of compliance with mandatory instructions would usually be impossible. The power of pressure groups, though not mandatory, can be similarly destructive of the real independence of the member.

The Constitution (article 27) also prohibits members from voting by proxy. Under the Fourth Republic, absenteeism was a regular thing. The French Parliamentary system makes no provision for pairing, and since the Assembly has been hitherto accustomed to voting a great many Bills every session, the obligation of personal voting would have been a much heavier burden on the French Deputy than it is on the member of the British House of Commons, though it would not have been so hard on his feet. Apart from votes by show of hands, or by standing, voting in the French Parliament is by ballot, and proxy-voting used to be general. Either one member of the group cast the votes for the whole group (the Communist method), or members gave a number of signed voting papers to one or more proxies, who voted on their behalf. If more than one proxy voted for the same member, the Secretaries detected it when the votes were checked. If the proxy voted in a way the member disliked, he could send in a *rectification de vote*. This did not affect the counting, but it often enabled a Deputy to save face if his vote had been cast in a way that his electors would dislike. One result of this system was that debates which were in actual fact conducted before almost empty benches could be followed by votes including upwards of 75 per cent of the membership of the House.

The Fifth Republic has changed all this. Henceforth a member may delegate his vote only for five reasons, duly notified in writing in advance. They are: absence on grounds of illness, accident or family circumstances; absence on a Government mission or on military service; absence from France on the occasion of an extraordinary session; or owing to representation of the Senate or the Assembly at a meeting of an international Assembly. No member may cast a proxy vote for more than one of his colleagues at a time. *Rectification de vote* is now prohibited.[1]

Under the Fifth Republic, the member is required, not only to vote in person, but to vote regularly. Parliamentary salaries have been increased, but the total is now divided into two parts: a basic salary, and an 'attendance bonus' (*indemnité de fonction*), which is received in full only if the member's attendance is satisfactory.[2] Each House is free to decide exactly how members are to be penalized for non-attendance. The Assembly's Standing Orders provide that absence from three consecutive Commission sittings without valid explanation entails the member's resignation from the Commission and the loss of a third of the attendance bonus, until the

[1] The Assembly now has electronic voting, each Deputy having his own apparatus and key. In practice, some Deputies surrender their keys to group leaders.

[2] The basic salary is the average salary of members of the highest category of the Civil Service (*hors échelle*). Under the Fourth Republic it was that of the *Conseillers d'Etat*. The attendance bonus is an innovation of the Fifth Republic. There was some criticism of the increased salaries, at a time when taxation was being increased and general wage increases discouraged. But it has been pointed out that the increased salary is taxed at a higher rate. Members are also not allowed to supplement their incomes, though certain exceptions are allowed, in particular the holding of military and civil pensions and receipt of the allowances paid to local government representatives.

opening of the following October session. Absence without valid
explanation from more than a third of the votes by ballot in any
month entails the loss of a third of the monthly attendance bonus
Two-thirds of the bonus is forfeited in the case of absence from
more than half the votes.[1]

The general organization of Parliamentary business

Members of Parliament are, in fact, being paid more for less work—
or perhaps more accurately for shorter hours—since, under th
Fifth Republic, Parliament sits for a maximum of five and a hal
months in the year, whereas during the later years of the Fourth
Republic it sat for a minimum of seven months. The Parliamentar
Commissions can meet when Parliament is not sitting, however
The first session, from the first Tuesday in October to the third
Friday in December, lasts 74 days and is intended to be mainly con
cerned with the budget. The second, from the end of April to July
may not exceed three months and is mainly concerned with th
legislative programme. Extraordinary sessions may be held onl
if convened by the President of the Republic, which means, i
effect, by the Prime Minister, since the President requires a counter
signature, or on the request of an absolute majority of the member
of the Assembly, for a specific agenda. In the latter case, the sessio
must be closed as soon as the agenda has been completed and, i
any case, after a period not exceeding 12 days.[2] In addition, Parlia

[1] During the first session (April to July 1959) from 75 to 100 Deputie
were fined. French ingenuity was already finding ways of getting round thi
unpopular provision, however. It was remarked that poorly attended debate
were often followed by an influx of voters, the qualification for the attendanc
bonus being presence for the *vote*, not for the debate. The 'valid explanation
proviso also enables Commissions to interpret the regulations very liberally.

[2] A final paragraph (article 29) states that a 'new session' may not be hel
until a month has elapsed after 'the closure decree', except on the request of th
Prime Minister. This has been interpreted (*v.* for instance, M. Duverge
op. cit., p. 114) as referring to the conditions governing the calling of an
extraordinary session. It would seem possible to take it to mean that a *secon
extraordinary session could be called only in these circumstances, but th
the condition did not apply to the calling of the first.

ment meets as of right on two occasions; after an election, for an
extraordinary session of up to a fortnight; and during a state of
emergency, as defined by article 16, when it continues to sit for
the duration of the emergency.[1]

At the beginning of the October session, each House elects its
bureau, consisting of the President, Vice-Presidents (six for the
Assembly and four for the Senate), Secretaries (12 for the Assembly
and eight for the Senate), whose job is to supervise the production
of the official records and check the votes, and the *Questeurs* (three
for each House), who are responsible for administrative and financial arrangements. With the exception of the President, the
members of the *bureau* are, in effect, chosen by the leaders of the
Parliamentary groups, the Assembly normally endorsing the list of
names presented by them. The functions of the *bureau* as a collective
body are to organize and supervise the different services in the
Assembly, and, if required, to advise the President on a number of
points, in particular on disciplinary matters and the admissibility of
Bills or resolutions.

The President of the Assembly is elected at the first meeting of the
session, which is presided over by the oldest member (*le doyen
d'âge*) Formerly elected annually, the President is now elected for
the duration of the Parliament.[2] The Constitution makes no mention of the system of election, which is unchanged. The ballot is
secret. For election at a first or second ballot, an absolute majority
of the membership of the House is required, but a relative majority
only is required at the third ballot. The President has certain new
functions under the Fifth Republic. He must be consulted by the
President of the Republic as to the existence of an emergency, as
defined by article 16. A private member's Bill or amendment which
the President of the Assembly believes to be constitutional, but
which the Government has challenged as unconstitutional, may be
submitted by him to the Constitutional Council. For the rest,

---

[1] *v. infra*, pp. 142–4.
[2] In the case of the President of the Senate, until the next partial renewal.
In other matters, the functions of the two Presidents are similar.

Presidents carry out the normal functions of Chairman. They do not have the unchallenged authority of the Speaker of the House of Commons, partly, though only partly, because they remain active members of their parties and partly, perhaps, because under the Fourth Republic they had to be re-elected annually by their colleagues, but they have a position of great prestige, the President of the Assembly ranking fourth in the order of precedence, immediately after the President of the Senate.[1]

Under the Fifth Republic, the Assembly's Standing Orders give somewhat more discretion to the President than his predecessors have had, particularly in calling Deputies to order, and in calling for the closure of debates, but it still remains to be seen how far these powers will be effectively translated from paper to practice.

French Parliamentary procedure has to take into account the existence of a number of Parliamentary groups, not always classifiable as belonging definitely to the Government or to the Opposition side. Only organized groups, that is, groups with 30 members or more, are now represented at the *Conférence des Présidents* and on the Parliamentary Commissions into which each House is divided for purposes of legislation. The traditional method of evading the regulations of minimum membership, by tacking on a number of isolated members, or small groups, for 'administrative purposes', is now prohibited.[2] Representation of groups on Commissions is

[1] But it is the President of the Senate who now replaces the President of the Republic, if incapacitated, and not the President of the Assembly, as under the Fourth Republic. One reason for the change may be that, since the Senate is renewed partially, there is always a President of the Senate in office. It is the President of the Assembly, however, who presides over a meeting of the two Houses in Congress at Versailles, if this procedure of constitutional revision is chosen in preference to a referendum.

[2] Under the previous régimes, the required number was 14. In 1958, it was raised to 28, but the provision had not entered into application by the time the Fourth Republic came to an end. The system of affiliated members or groups benefited both affiliates (*apparentés*) and parent group, since it enabled both to enjoy the advantages of parliamentary groups without fulfilling the obligation to accept a common policy—which involved no more than subscribing to a vaguely worded declaration.

oportional to their strength in the Assembly including affiliates
pparentés). Isolated members can be members of Commissions
ly if elected by the whole Assembly to any vacancies remaining
:er the seats have been allotted to group members.

The Parliamentary timetable is drawn up every week by *la
nférence des Présidents*—a meeting of the President and Vice-
esidents of the Assembly, and of heads of Parliamentary groups,
esidents of Commissions, and the *rapporteur général* of the
nance Commission. Voting in this body is weighted in proportion
party strength. What influence the Government used to have on
decisions depended largely on the prestige of the Government
d on the persuasiveness of the Government representatives. The
w Constitution gives the Government effective control over the
netable by according priority to Government Bills and to those
ivate members' Bills acceptable to the Government.

Legislative procedure

lls may be introduced and have their first reading in either House,
cept for Finance Bills, which must be read first in the National
ssembly. Private members' Bills are not in order if they involve a
crease in the revenue or an increase in expenditure. Once intro-
iced, Bills are submitted either to one of the six regular Com-
issions, or, on the request of either Government or Assembly, to
ad hoc Commission whose members may not exceed 30. Com-
issions formerly numbered 19, each consisting of 44 members.
ie purpose of the reduction is twofold: to reduce the authority
' Commissions, whose Presidents, when the field of activity of
ommissions roughly coincided with that of a Ministry, tended to
come shadow Ministers; and also to prevent the time-wasting
ocess of submitting to several Commissions Bills whose scope
such as to interest more than one Ministry, the main Commission
maining responsible for the report, the others merely stating their
)inion. For instance, the Bill to ratify the E.D.C. Treaty in 1954
as submitted to the Foreign Affairs Commission for report, and
so to four other Commissions for their opinion. Nevertheless,

G

the Standing Orders also decided that the practice of submittir
Bills to more than one Commission should be continued.

The Assembly normally sits on four afternoons a week, Con
missions holding meetings in the morning. The Friday sessions a
normally reserved for questions. Debate on a Government Bill b
gins with a Ministerial declaration, followed by the Commission
report. Formerly, the Assembly debate normally[1] took place on t
basis of the Commission's amended text, and not on the Gover
ment's Bill, and the Commission, not the Minister, was responsib
for piloting the Bill through the House. The Government was ev
unable to propose its own counter-amendments, except by devio
procedures such as issuing so-called 'corrected' versions of
article, or getting a Deputy to move an amendment from the floo

The new Constitution changes all that. Henceforth the Minist
pilots his own Bill when it comes before the House, and may pr
pose amendments, and object to the proposal of amendments fro
the floor. The probable effect of these changes on the authority ar
stability of Governments will be discussed in the following chapte
As far as legislative procedure is concerned, the right of Gover
ments to refuse to consider amendments not previously submitt
to the relevant Commission, to insist on a single vote on the whol
or a part of the Bill, including only such amendments as have be
either proposed or accepted by the Government, the further restri
tions on amendments introduced by the Standing Orders and t
right of the President to call for the closure, when, in his view, t
case for and against has been adequately presented, could, if pr
perly used, produce far more coherent and orderly debates, ar
consequently better drafted laws. It remains to be seen, howeve
how these new provisions work in practice.

The Assembly first debates the general principles of the Bi
as presented by the Government and the Commission spokesma

[1] A great many Bills are adopted without debate, particularly priva
members' Bills. If there is a debate on these, it is still on the basis of t
Commission's report and the Government spokesman takes part only if he
desires.

d then votes on it article by article, finally voting on the text as
whole, as amended. This completes what is called the first reading.
he Bill then goes to the Senate (or to the Assembly if it has been
ad first in the Senate) where it goes through a similar process. If
ssed by both Houses, it is promulgated by the President of the
epublic and published in the *Journal Officiel* and is then law.[1]

During the debate, Ministers and Presidents of Commissions may
tervene at any moment; Deputies may interrupt a speaker, with
s permission, for a maximum of five minutes, or may rise on a
oint of order at any time. Ministers may be present at debates and
eak in either House as was the practice under previous régimes.
he debate may be open or 'organized'. In the first case, would-
speakers notify the President, who chooses the order in which
ey are called. In the second case, the total time allotted to the
ebate and the share allotted to each Parliamentary group (which is
roportional to its strength in the House) is rigidly worked out in
dvance (though often less rigidly adhered to). An innovation of the
ifth Republic is the requirement in the Standing Orders, so far
idely ignored in practice, that Deputies shall not read their
eeches. Before the vote is taken, spokesmen of groups who wish
explain why their groups have decided to vote one way or the
her are normally allowed five minutes in which to do so (*l'expli-
tion de vote*).[2]

Finance and Organic laws

he voting of Finance and Organic laws is subject to special pro-
dures laid down in the Constitution. An 'organic law' is one of
vo things. It is either one of the 19, which the Constitution pro-
ded for in order to complete a number of its provisions, and which
ere promulgated as Ordinances (*Ordonnances portant loi organique*)
uring the transitional period when the Government had full
owers; or else it is that provided for under article 34, to 'complete

[1] Promulgation takes place within 15 days unless, within that period, the
esident asks Parliament to reconsider the Bill. Parliament must comply
ith this request.   [2] On voting procedure, *v. supra*, pp. 92–3.

and define' the legislative powers of Parliament and which at t
time of writing had not seen the light. This must be voted accor
ing to the procedure required for the amendment of all 20 organ
laws. Though these organic laws may be amended, no new on
can be voted.[1] The essential difference between this procedure a
the normal legislative procedure is that Bills must be tabled a f
fortnight before they are debated and that, if the two Houses di
agree, the Assembly can override the Senate only by voting t
law by an absolute majority of its membership, and then only
the Prime Minister requests it to do so. Organic laws affecting t
Senate must be voted in the same terms by both Houses. Organ
laws are promulgated only when the Constitutional Council h
declared that they are in conformity with the Constitution.

The procedure for voting Finance Bills is designed to preve
the Assembly from using delaying tactics, as it did under the Four
Republic, in order to bring pressure to bear on Governments.
the Assembly has not completed the first reading within 40 days, t
Government asks the Senate to read the Bill first, and to comple
its reading within a fortnight. If the Bill has not been voted aft
70 days, the Government may apply its provisions by Ordinanc
If the Government has failed to introduce the Bill in time for it
be promulgated by the beginning of the financial year, it may a
Parliament to authorize taxation by decree and to authorize e
penditure in respect of any estimates previously accepted I
the Assembly. The authorization may be asked for in one of tw
ways. Either the Assembly is requested, ten days before the end
the session, to vote the parts of the law covering the collection
taxes and the general headings of expenditure, the text then bein
submitted to the Senate as a matter of urgency;[2] or else if this fai
the Assembly is requested, two days before the end of the session,
vote a special Bill entitling the Government to collect taxes in antic

---

[1] But v. p. 108 n.1.

[2] When a matter is declared 'urgent' the procedure is speeded up. In pra
tice, this procedure has been used only rarely except during the early years
the Fourth Republic.

ation of authorization by the finance law. This Bill also is treated
, a matter of urgency.

These provisions cannot, of course, ensure that the Assembly
ill accede to the request, in which case the Government is no
etter off than Governments of the Fourth Republic were at times—
or instance, when the Assembly voted expenditure, but refused to
ote the parts of the Bill providing for the necessary revenue. The
moral here is, perhaps, that Governments should present their
udgets on time! Nor can they ensure that the Assembly, if it does
ote the Bill, will do so without amending it in ways displeasing to
he Government, though, if the Government decides to make the
sue a matter of confidence, the Assembly may hesitate to turn
he Government out, particularly if the consequence may be a dis-
olution. The implications of these provisions, in the context of the
eneral relationship between Government and Parliament, will be
iscussed in the following chapter.

It will have been noted that Finance Bills are normally voted by
he two Houses, though the Constitution (article 39) requires them
o be voted first by the Assembly. There is nothing in French
Parliamentary procedure comparable to the British system, which
ermits the House of Commons to override the House of Lords in
he matter of Money Bills more easily than in the matter of ordinary
egislation.[1] In France, if the two Houses disagree on a Finance Bill,
he procedure is the same as that governing disagreements on
organic Bills.

Relations between the two Houses

The 1958 Constitution does not permit the Assembly to override
he Senate, as it could under the previous Constitution, unless the
Government decides to intervene on the side of the Assembly. If
he Government does not intervene, a Bill on which the two Houses
disagree can go back and forth between Assembly and Senate—the

[1] There were slight differences between procedure governing finance Bills
nd that governing other Bills under the Fourth Republic. The Senate was
iven a shorter time to consider finance Bills.

process known as 'the shuttle' (*la navette*)—indefinitely. Second, and if necessary, further readings deal only with articles on which agreement has still not been reached. There is no provision in the Constitution for putting an end to persistent disagreement.

If, however, the Government does intervene, it may do so either passively or actively. In the first case, it may, after the Bill has been read twice in each House, require the setting-up of a Commission consisting of equal numbers (seven) from each House and, if the Commission reaches agreement, the Bill may then be submitted by the Government to both Houses to be voted on (with only such amendments as the Government accepts). If the Commission does not agree, or if the Bill as agreed is rejected by either House, the two Houses may make further efforts to agree, or drop the Bill, or shelve it. Alternatively, the Government may intervene actively with a request, first, to each House to give the Bill a further reading and then, if the disagreement persists, to the Assembly to vote either on the Commission's Bill, or on its own Bill, with or without any amendments proposed by the Senate. In order to override the Senate, the Bill (unless finance or organic) requires only an ordinary majority vote in the Assembly.

This means, of course, that, where the Government is not interested in a Bill, the co-ordinate relationship between the two Houses which existed under the 1875 Constitution is restored and the Senate can effectively block legislation proposed by the Assembly.

Except for this contingent legislative equality, and its effective right of veto over any change in its own status (which existed also under the 1946 Constitution), the Senate remains a subordinate legislative Chamber. The Government is not responsible to it. The prestige of the Senate is, however, increased in several ways, some of which have already been mentioned.[1] During the first year of the

[1] They include the right of the President of the Senate to replace the President of the Republic, if incapacitated, until the election of a new President; the obligation on the President to consult the President of the Senate before applying article 16, and before deciding on the desirability of a dissolution.

ew régime, its prestige was derived, in practice, less from any
onstitutional provisions than from the election to the Senate of a
umber of Parliamentary personalities who had been defeated in
he elections to the Assembly, at a time when the Assembly included
n almost unprecedented number of rather nondescript newcomers.

Restrictions on Parliamentary sovereignty

a) THE LEGISLATIVE SPHERE. One of the most important innova-
ions of the Fifth Republic is the restriction of the scope of Parliamentary activity. This represents a break with the Republican
radition of Parliamentary sovereignty.

Parliament is henceforth regarded as having two functions: that
of legislating within a circumscribed field and that of supervision
nd control of the Government.[1] The Government, on the other
and, while it retains the traditional functions belonging to the
xecutive, henceforth deals, by executive action, with all matters not
pecifically reserved to the legislature and may also, with the per-
nission of Parliament, take over, for a limited period, responsibility
or dealing with matters defined by the Constitution as properly
elonging to the legislature (article 38).

e right of the President of the Senate to submit Bills in certain circumstances
o the Constitutional Council and (like the President of the Assembly) to
nominate three members of the Constitutional Council; the right of the Senate
o equal representation with the Assembly in the Senate of the Community
nd in the High Court of Justice, the need for the Assembly to obtain the concurrence of the Senate before requesting a referendum and the right of the
Senate to receive Presidential messages.

The right of the Prime Minister to request the approval of the Senate at
ny time he so desires (article 49) existed also under the Fourth Republic. It
s difficult to see why a Prime Minister should take advantage of the opportunity unless he is seeking to play off one House against the other, for, though
he Government is not constitutionally obliged to resign if defeated in the
Senate, not to do so would entail some loss of face. This view is borne out by
several passages in M. Debré's speech to the *Conseil d'Etat* (*v. Revue fran-
aise de Science Politique*, March 1959, pp. 8, 17, 26).

[1] A third function should be mentioned: a declaration of war must be
authorized by Parliament (article 35).

There is, of course, nothing new in the exercise of legislativ functions by Governments. *Décrets-lois* of the Third Republi *lois-cadres* and special powers under the Fourth Republic, were a instances of delegated legislation. The difference is that, hithert such delegated legislation has been regarded as exceptional, the ru of Parliamentary sovereignty being maintained in principle; it h also been temporary, Parliament being the final judge of the exter and the duration of special powers accorded to Governments t legislate by decree; and it has been subject to ratification by Parli ment.

This is, in fact, the first serious attempt in French Republica history to define a 'legislative sphere' (*le domaine de la loi*). Certai matters have been, in the past, constitutionally reserved to the legis lature, others have been so reserved by custom, or by virtue c special legislative provisions. For instance, the choice of elector systems, the granting of amnesties, questions concerning the funda mental rights and liberties of the citizen, property, personal status penal law, the principles of taxation, and so on, are all matters tha the legislature has normally claimed the right to deal with. But thes traditions constitute restrictions of the executive's right to encroac on the legislature. The legislative domain had been, up to now, any thing claimed by Parliament as such.

> The sphere assigned to legislation by the Constitution and b custom is merely a minimum guaranteed sphere. Beyond stretches an *a priori*, unlimited, and indeterminate field of actio for the unfettered initiative of the legislator who, by legislatin on any matter whatsoever, thereby incorporates it in the legis lative sphere.[1]

[1] Georges Galichon, *Aspects de la Procédure législative en France* (*Revu française de Science Politique*, October–December 1954, p. 795). Cf. Pint *Eléments de Droit Constitutionnel* (Lille, 1952), p. 516: 'The Constitution doe not define the legislative sphere. It does not limit the matters that can be dea with by legislation', and also the following extract from a speech in the Sena by M. Léo Hamon on 25th January 1951:—'French law recognizes no suc thing as a "law", in the sense in which it exists in a rigid Constitution of th

To prescribe limits to legislative activity, leaving everything out-side these limits to the executive, is, therefore, something quite new in Republican history.[1]

As defined by article 34 of the Constitution, the field of legis-lation now includes two categories. The first consists of the 'rules governing' certain enumerated subjects—the fundamental liberties of the citizen, civil status and civic rights, liability to taxation and national defence, the penal code, amnesty, declarations of war, electoral laws, the creation of nationalized industries . . . to quote the main ones listed. The second consists of the 'general principles governing' the organization of a further list of subjects—national defence, local Government, education, property and commercial rights, labour, trade union and social security, finance laws (in con-ditions defined in an organic law) and 'programme-laws'[2] in the field of economic and social policy. . . . Everything else belongs to the executive field (article 37).[3]

The list certainly still gives scope for a good deal of Parliamentary activity. Unfortunately, it also gives scope for a great deal of argu-ment, both regarding the respective spheres of executive and legis-lative action, in general, and also regarding the distinction between

American type, where a Constitutional Court ensures respect even by Parlia-ment for the separation of functions. In this country, a law is not defined in relation to the matters with which it deals; the definition is juridically speak-ing, purely formal: a law is an act emanting from Parliament.'

[1] The law of the 17th August 1948 did attempt to define a field of activity that could properly be described as executive. But this was, in fact, a piece of special pleading designed to get round the Constitutional prohibition (under article 13) of delegated legislation, without having recourse to a revision of the Constitution.

[2] A 'programme-law' is an innovation of the Fifth Republic—it is a long-term project and Parliament is assumed to be morally committed to vote later instalments of expenditure in application of its provisions, as they turn up in subsequent budgets.

[3] It should be noted, however, that, under article 85, the constitutional status of member-States of the Community can be revised by an ordinary law with the assent of the Senate of the Community. This constitutes, in a sense, a third category.

general principles, which, in the second category, alone belong to the legislative field, and the detailed application, which is now a matter for the executive. 'One man's detail may honestly be another man's principle.'[1]

There is scope for argument, too, regarding the respective functions of the two organs to which the Constitution entrusts decisions affecting the application of the new principles. No doubt, these problems will be resolved in time. Some of them are worth mentioning, however, because they raise important issues in themselves, and also because they illustrate very clearly the kind of uncertainty that has been created by the numerous omissions and ambiguities of this badly drafted Constitution. The title of 'the worst drafted article of a Constitution that does no credit to the French language'[2] has already been claimed for article 89, governing the conditions of Constitutional revision. Articles 34, 37 and 41, have certainly an equally strong claim to consideration.

The Constitution provides (article 37) that, in the case of laws passed *before* the new Constitution came into force, the *Conseil d'Etat*—the supreme administrative jurisdiction[3]—must be consulted as to whether or not they now come within the executive field. Those that do can henceforth be modified by decree.[4] In the case of laws passed *since* the Constitution came into force, the Constitutional Council will decide whether a matter has erroneously been treated as within the legislative field, when it would properly come within the executive field. Without the Constitutional Council's authorization, Governments cannot themselves act on this assumption and proceed to modify by decree what is, in form, a law.

[1] Martin Harrison, *The Constitution of the Fifth Republic* in *Political Studies*, February 1959, p. 49.   [2] M. Duverger, op. cit., p. 138.

[3] On the functions of the *Conseil d'Etat*, *v*. the author's *France—the Fourth Republic*, pp. 105–10, 138–9, and Brian Chapman, *The Profession of Government* (Allen and Unwin, 1958).

[4] The *Conseil d'Etat's* rôle is purely advisory, however. On this, *v*. G. Morange, *La hiérarchie des textes dans la Constitution de 1958*, in *Recueil Dalloz hebdomadaire*, 28th January 1959.

So far the position, though complicated, is relatively clear. What is not clear is exactly how the propriety of a Government's action can be challenged, if it proceeds to decide for itself to treat, as a matter suitable for executive action, something that might be regarded by others as falling within the legislative sphere. Article 41 permits the Government to object to a Bill or an amendment, on the ground that the subject is not a proper one for legislation, and if the President of the relevant House disagrees, the matter is submitted to the Constitutional Council. The President of the Republic, or the President of either Assembly, can submit any Bill for the Constitutional Council's ruling as to its conformity with the Constitution (article 51). There is no Constitutional provision enabling Parliament to object to a Government decree, on the ground that the Constitution required its subject matter to be dealt with by a law and not by a decree.

It has been suggested that injured parties have redress *via* the normal channels of administrative law. The *Conseil d'Etat* can decide whether to admit an appeal by a citizen against the application to him of a decree, on the ground that the Government was not entitle to issue it. Three objections might be raised to this procedure. First, it is a long, slow and chancy method; second, it raises a fresh problem, that of the propriety of a decision by the *Conseil d'Etat*, on the grounds not of the legality, but of the constitutionality of the Government's position, a subject on which decision belongs properly to the Constitutional Council and not to the *Conseil d'Etat*; and third, even if the procedure is admitted, it is likely to result in conflicting decisions by the *Conseil d'Etat* and the Constitutional Council, since the Government, if faced with an adverse decision by the *Conseil d'Etat* can retaliate by appealing to the Constitutional Council to declare unconstitutional the Bill forced upon it by the decision of the *Conseil d'Etat*. The conflict would, of necessity, be short-lived, since the Constitutional Council's decision is final, but the intervening period could be extremely confusing and conflicting decisions could persist on, for instance, pre- and post-1958 laws dealing with the same subject.

These are some of the questions that lawyers are asking themselves. A politician or a political scientist thinks rather in terms of political remedies, and on this at least two points spring to mind. The first is that, if Parliament feels strongly on the matter, it can defeat the Government by a vote of censure, and then ensure that its successor regularizes the situation (always assuming that the President does not step in and call for a dissolution). But this may be a costly step to deal with a problem whose importance might lie less in any individual case, than in an *accumulation* leading to progressive encroachment by the executive on the legislative sphere. One of the chief criticisms of the 1958 Constitution is, precisely, that it overlooks the need to provide adequate safety-valves for opposition falling short of a desire to turn the Government out. The second point that seems relevant to the problem is that, unless the challengeable executive action is such as to attract public attention, encroachment by the executive could be imperceptible for a considerable time. This point is also relevant to the suggestion that the *Conseil d'Etat* can intervene on behalf of the citizen. It can do so, if at all, only if the citizen himself appeals, as an injured party, to an administrative tribunal. Failing this, there seems as yet no way of preventing executive encroachment.

It is possible that some of the uncertainty may be dissipated by the organic law, which article 34 provides for, in order to 'complete and define' its provisions. That provision, in turn, has uncertainties and ambiguities of its own which cannot be gone into here.[1]

Two arguments in particular have been put forward in support of

[1] It has been suggested, for instance, that the Constitution authorizes only *one* organic law and that, therefore, this would not be subject to amendment; that the term 'completed and defined' is limitative and would permit only such changes in the present text as are needed to make the original intentions plain—in other words, that the organic law could not 'complete' the list of legislative functions by adding others to them, an interpretation that could result in an encroachment (or successive encroachments), by the legislature on what was originally intended to be the field of action of the executive. The question will be, in fact, decided by the Constitutional Council, which may interpret the Constitution either restrictively or liberally.

the restrictions on the legislative activity of Parliament. The first is that they reverse the tendency to *gouvernement d'assemblée* which, with a divided Assembly such as existed throughout most of the life of the Fourth Republic, meant that Governments had to fight inch by inch in order to survive, and that, more often than not, the price of survival was inaction. The second is that, in an age of wholesale Governmental intervention in economic and social life, some degree of delegated legislation is essential and that French Parliaments have for too long resisted this necessary evolution. It was generally admitted by critics of the post-war Parliamentary system that Parliament legislated too much and that there was far too much detailed and unco-ordinated legislation.[1] A Radical Deputy wrote in 1956 that the Assembly was sovereign, chaotic and tyrannical, and by making everything its business failed to do anything properly. M. Debré accused Parliaments of the Fourth Republic of 'a two-fold deviation'. Since the war, in particular, he said, they had witnessed:

a Parliament snowed under by Bills, and seeking to multiply interventions haphazard on points of detail, and a Govern-

[1] During the first Parliament of the Fourth Republic (January 1947 to June 1951) 1,289 Bills were passed (of which 937 were Government Bills); during the first half of the second Parliament (June 1951 to August 1953) 452 (of which 299 were Government Bills). These figures alone do not give an accurate impression of the legislative activity of Parliament, since they leave out of account Bills that were defeated and the very much larger number (about half of those introduced) which never got beyond the stage of being considered by the relevant Commission. Mr. Lidderdale (*The Parliament of France*, Hansard Society, 1949, p. 179) estimates that in the 1946–7 session, only one in 17 of the private members' Bills reached the Statute Book. Mr. Harrison (op cit., p. 50) estimates that, towards the end of the Fourth Republic, about 1,800 Bills were presented during a session, of which 750 were rejected and 250 debated.

Cf. also André Philip (*La Crise de la démocratie française, Preuves*, November 1958, p. 13) on this point. The Assembly, he says, passed about 300–500 Bills a year, for the most part dealing with matters more suitable to a *Conseil Général*, while no serious discussion took place on the plan for the country's general economic policy.

ment on the other hand, dealing with the most serious national problems without interference by Parliament.

It is possible, however, that the Fifth Republic has gone too far in the opposite direction and, by giving Parliament too little business, reduced both its incentive to efficiency and its capacity to ensure that of the Government in the fields in which the latter now replaces Parliament.

(b) THE SUPERVISION OF CONSTITUTIONALITY AND OF ELECTIONS. The Constitutional Council also limits Parliamentary sovereignty since, hitherto, Parliament has been, in effect, the sole judge of the constitutionality of its acts. Under the Fourth Republic, it was possible for the Council of the Republic (acting conjointly with the President of the Republic, that is, presumably by agreement with the Government, since the President required a counter-signature) to bring allegedly unconstitutional legislation to the notice of the Constitutional Committee. The procedure was used only once, however, and then on a matter of no importance. Where the two Houses were agreed, there was no machinery for challenging the constitutionality of legislation.

The withdrawal from Parliament of the right to decide disputed elections is also a limitation on Parliament, but one that many people would applaud, since the Assembly has been guilty of extremely partisan and illogical decisions. The Constitutional Council is now responsible for dealing with these disputes.

What will affect Parliament's position far more than the Constitutional provisions themselves is the spirit in which they are applied. That is something which will depend partly on the attitude of Deputies themselves, on the extent to which they accept, or reject, or use ingenuity to modify, the rôle that they are intended to play. They could, for instance, use much more intelligently than they do the technique of the Parliamentary Question. One Algerian Deputy has already shown the way.[1] Much will depend on the extent to which they can overcome their divisions suffi-

[1] v. infra, p. 184.

ciently to acquire any coherent or consistent conception of what their own functions ought to be. It will depend, too, on the spirit in which the Constitutional Council interprets the problems submitted to it. But most of all, it will depend on the extent to which Government and Assembly can establish some kind of working relationship which does not, in the effort to end the Parliamentary domination characteristic of the Fourth Republic, go too far in the opposite direction, and by reducing Parliament to a state of humiliation and frustration, produce either the atrophy of Parliamentary institutions themselves, or else an explosion and yet another reaction in the long series of actions and reactions since 1789.

CHAPTER VII

The Relations between Government and Parliament

The purpose of the Constitution

The 1958 Constitution deliberately seeks to change the focus of interest in French political life. Traditionally, the popularly elected Assembly has been the maker and breaker of Governments. Except for the rare occurrence of a dissolution, which happened only twice in 83 years, Deputies could count on remaining for the five years (or four, under the Third Republic) of their term of office, however many Governments came and went. Under the Fifth Republic, the focus of interest is the executive, that is the President of the Republic and the Government. The Constitution seeks to strengthen Governments, not merely by limiting the scope of Parliamentary activities, in the hope of reducing the number of issues and occasions on which Governments can come into conflict with the Assembly, but also by carefully defining and limiting the conditions in which Governments can be defeated.

Both these methods are essentially attempts to eliminate the symptoms of the disease of Governmental instability, without sacrificing the essential condition of Parliamentary government, the responsibility of the Government to the popularly elected Assembly. When Parliament is a framework within which one of two parties governs with the consent of the other, which hopes and strives to replace it, strong government and Parliamentary government can coexist harmoniously, because the Government is at the same time the leader and the emanation of the Parliamentary majority. That being so, there can normally be no conflict between Parliament and Government on the issues of policy that divide Government and Opposition, since 'Parliament' means the majority party, which is linked to the Government by common interests. Both Government and Opposition have a common interest, too, in accepting the same rules of the Parliamentary game.

This classic picture of the two-party system as it works in Great Britain has little, if any, relevance to the problems that beset French Governments in their relations with Parliament. The essential difference is not that France has a multi-party system. Multi-party systems are the rule rather than the exception in countries with Parliamentary government, and many countries have been able to combine strong government with a Parliamentary system. The French system has two essential characteristics which make the combination difficult and sometimes impossible. First, neither on the Government nor on the Opposition side do parties normally have sufficient common interest to hold them together for long. There is, therefore, no clear dividing line between Government and Opposition, and majorities can, and very often do, shift during the life of a Parliament, so that there can be first Left and then Right Governments within the life-time of the same Parliament. Second, the presence since the war of a large permanent opposition to the régime, which includes Communists on the one hand and anti-Communists, sometimes extremely right-wing, on the other, has often meant that a small—sometimes a very small—number of additional opposition votes could bring down a Government. But since the Opposition was both a temporary combination and a politically heterogeneous one, the defeat could not entail a whole-sale change of either Government personnel or policy. The parties (or most of them) that formed the preceding coalition returned to office, either giving way to the majority on the particular issue that defeated them, or changing their political mixture just enough to enable them to obtain a majority. In either case, this situation in-volved domination of the Government by an Assembly in which

H

opposition elements could combine to defeat Governments but not to replace them.

The authors of the 1958 Constitution, and in particular, the first Prime Minister of the new régime, M. Debré, deliberately set out to overcome these obstacles to stable government by substituting for the common interest of disciplined parties a series of rigid rules.[1] Constitutional rules have been designed to make it more difficult for Governments to be defeated; changes in procedure are intended to prevent Governments from being harassed and subjected to constant pressure by the Assembly; and the Government is given, in addition, weapons intended to enable it either to ignore Parliamentary pressure, or else to make its consequences unpleasant for Deputies.

The Constitutional methods of ensuring Governmental responsibility

The Constitution lays down three methods of enforcing Governmental responsibility to Parliament. The first decisions of the Constitutional Council make it quite clear that, in the opinion of its present members, these are intended to be the sole ways in which Governments can henceforth be defeated.

First, the Assembly can defeat the Government either on its programme or on a declaration of general policy. The wording of this sentence (article 49) is ambiguous. It merely states that:

> After discussion in the Council of Ministers, the Prime Minister pledges the responsibility of his Government on his programme or possibly on a declaration of general policy.

No special procedure is laid down. No occasion or time limit is mentioned. It has so far been generally understood that the submission of the Prime Minister's programme would take place at the

[1] *v.* Speech by M. Debré to the *Conseil d'Etat* on 27th August 1959:
'The draft Constitution, drawn up in the light of a long and costly experience, includes certain precise procedural mechanisms, which would be out of place in a document of this kind, were it not for our realization that they are necessary in order to change our habits. To break bad habits, strict rules are required.' (*Revue française de Science Politique*, March 1959, p. 14.)

beginning of the Government's period of office. The first Prime Minister did so submit his Government's programme. If this precedent is followed, it constitutes a partial return to the practice of the Third Republic, when newly appointed Prime Ministers asked for the confidence of the Chamber of Deputies, both in their programme and in the composition of their Government.[1] If confidence is withheld, the Government resigns. Since no special procedure is mentioned, a majority of those voting is sufficient. A 'declaration of general policy' is generally assumed to be some kind of re-statement of the Government's programme which a Prime Minister might find it expedient to make, as, for instance, after a Government reshuffle. Such a declaration was made for the first time in October 1959.[2]

Second, the Assembly can defeat the Government by passing a vote of censure. A motion of censure must be signed by at least a tenth of the members of the National Assembly; the vote takes place not less than 48 hours after the motion has been tabled; and only the votes of those favourable to the motion are counted. The

[1] The essential difference between this procedure and that of the previous régime is that Prime Ministers under the Fourth Republic were designated (désignés) by the President of the Republic and their official appointment by him followed their *investiture* by a majority vote in the Assembly. (Up to 1954 an absolute majority of the effective membership was required). The Prime Minister did not submit himself with his Ministers, but alone, though, from 1954 onwards, the names of Ministers were communicated to the Assembly before the investiture debate. The intention of the investiture procedure was to emphasize the need for the Prime Minister to satisfy the Assembly and also to emphasize the prestige of the Prime Minister within the Government.

[2] There was a request by some party spokesmen for a vote following the Foreign Minister's declaration at the end of April 1959. The Prime Minister was opposed to a vote, on the ground that the declaration was not one of general, but only of foreign policy. Following General de Gaulle's statement of France's Algerian policy on 16th September 1959, the Assembly, at the opening of the October session, debated a general declaration of the Government's Algerian and foreign policies. The procedure adopted was that, after the Prime Minister's speech, the President of the Assembly announced the Government's decision to 'pledge its responsibility' on these issues.

motion is carried, only if it receives the votes of an absolute majority of the effective membership of the Assembly. If it is defeated, the signatories cannot sign another motion of censure for the rest of the session.

Third, the Prime Minister (again after discussion in the Council of Ministers) may make an issue a matter of confidence. If he does so, confidence is presumed to have been accorded, and the proposal in question is presumed to have been carried, without a vote being taken, unless a motion of censure is tabled within 24 hours. A motion of censure is tabled, and voted on, in the same conditions as a motion of censure on the Government's general policy, though there is no limit to the number of censure motions that may be presented by the same Deputies on matters which the Government has made questions of confidence.

Responsibility in theory and in practice

These provisions call for several comments. The idea that a ration of one (unsuccessful) motion of censure per Deputy per session is likely to decrease the frequency of Government defeats is implausible, and this was not the real purpose of the rule. It was intended rather to prevent the use of motions of censure by a small number of Deputies either for propaganda purposes or as part of a general tactic of obstruction.[1] Deputies have still considerable elbow-room to defeat Governments, since there is no restriction on the number of censure motions relating to issues that the Government has made questions of confidence. What the procedure does put a stop to is the possibility that a Government may see its Bill defeated while it retains, constitutionally speaking, the confidence of the

[1] The measure was probably partly inspired by the desire to prevent the kind of Communist obstruction that occurred regularly in the early years of the Fourth Republic. In the first Assembly of the present régime, the Communists numbered only ten and so could not alone table a motion of censure, but at the time when the Constitution was drawn up it was generally estimated that they would number about 50, or somewhere in the region of a tenth of the Assembly.

Assembly. Under the Fourth Republic this was possible, and some-times happened, because only a majority of those voting was re-quired to defeat a Bill, while a majority of the effective membership of the Assembly was required to defeat a Government. Henceforth, the Government is in a position to say: 'Love me, love my Bill.'

This point may seem trivial to some British readers, since nothing, of course, obliged Prime Ministers of the Fourth Republic to stay in office in such a humiliating situation. But, as has already been pointed out, the resignation of a Prime Minister in the situation of Parliamentary deadlock that existed throughout most of the life of the Fourth Republic often achieved nothing, since his coalition or one very like it, was often the only one to be able to command a positive majority in the Assembly. In such circumstances his resigna-tion merely added to existing difficulties that of a long Govern-mental interregnum, at the end of which he might find himself back where he started from. The new procedure means that Govern-ments will be *obliged* to resign if the Assembly does not allow them to carry out their programme. The assumption henceforth is that those who are not prepared to turn a Government out must let it get on with its job.

The rules are rigid, in the sense that Governments can be defeated only on a limited number of occasions, and by a special procedure. It will therefore be virtually impossible for such defeats to occur on snap votes, or as a result of a Parliamentary storm that blows up unexpectedly. But the rules are not rigid in the sense that they place any real obstacles in the way of an Assembly which has de-cided that it does want to get rid of a Government. They do not, however, affect what have been, since the war, the most frequent causes of Governmental instability. Of the twenty Governments of the Fourth Republic (leaving that headed by General de Gaulle out of account) only five resigned because they were constitutionally obliged to do so. Of the rest, eight resigned without being defeated at all, and seven resigned in circumstances in which, under the pre-sent Constitution (as under the last) Governments would be constitutionally entitled to remain in power.

Constitutions cannot impose unity and discipline, if none exists. Nor can they, with impunity, make too violent a break with tradition. It may be asked whether, if circumstances return to normal, Deputies will for long tolerate a system which allows a Bill to be passed without the Assembly's having voted on it at all.

Parliamentary control and Parliamentary pressure

Parliament carries out its work of supervising the Government in three main ways. During sessions, opportunity is provided for exchanges of opinion during debates, but the main method of supervision is during the first stage of legislative procedure, by the examination of Bills in Commission. All members of recognized Parliamentary groups are members of a Commission (though not of more than one). The permanent Commissions in France have been extremely powerful bodies, able to summon both Civil Servants and Ministers before them to provide explanations and justification of measures being discussed in Commission. Since 1956, the powers of the Finance Commission, in particular, have been extensive.

In addition to the permanent Commissions, there are special Commissions (each with not more than thirty members, of whom not more than fifteen may be drawn from the same permanent Commission) to which Bills may be sent instead of to one of the permanent Commissions. The Assembly may itself ask for this procedure to be adopted. There are also Commissions of Enquiry, equivalent to Select Committees of the House of Commons, and Supervisory Commissions (*Commissions de Contrôle*), which supervise the management and finances of nationalized industries and public services. When Parliament is not sitting, Commissions may meet, though only if convened by their President, on the request of their *bureau*.

Information can also be obtained by individual Deputies by putting either written or oral questions to the relevant Minister. Questions on general policy are addressed to the Prime Minister.

Written questions are printed in the *Journal Officiel*. Ministers are (theoretically) bound to reply within a month, and their replies are printed in the *Journal Officiel*. They may, however, delay their reply for one, and sometimes two, months, and they are free to refuse to reply on the ground that to do so would be contrary to the public interest. If replies are unduly delayed, the President of the Assembly can ask the author whether he would prefer to put his question orally.

Oral questions may be with or without debate.[1] Ministers reply to them at a sitting reserved for this purpose once a week (in the Assembly, Friday afternoons). Questions without debate are called by the President and the questioner is allowed to speak for five minutes following the Minister's reply. The Minister may reply to this. No other speeches are allowed. Questions with debate are put by the questioner in a speech which may last up to half an hour. After the Minister's reply, the President may allow other members to speak for a period not exceeding fifteen minutes each. The Minister may give a final reply, if he so desires.

Oral questions with debate formed the subject of the first major battle between Parliament and Government, because, as is evident from the foregoing brief description, they could have become an instrument of pressure on the Government if, as the Standing Orders originally provided, the debate had concluded with a resolution and a vote. The Constitution of 1958 attempts to draw a clear line between the search for information and the exercise of pressure. It does so in two ways, the first positive, by modifications of legislative procedure, the second, negative, being the refusal to allow a technique intended for the provision of information (oral questions with debate) to be used in effect as an instrument of pressure. As the Prime Minister, M. Debré, put it, the Government did not intend to be faced every Friday with an implicit vote of confidence. Votes on a resolution, whether or not it followed an oral question with debate, could not, of course, constitutionally, have

---

[1] Under the Fourth Republic, oral questions with debate existed only in the Senate and then only from 1948 onwards.

defeated a Government. But such votes could have ended by weakening its authority.

The battle between Parliament and Government took place because the wording of the Constitution on this point, as on so many others, gave no clear guidance regarding the constitutionality of votes on resolutions and oral questions with debate. Assembly and Senate, therefore, at first included in their provisional Standing Orders articles permitting both.[1] The Constitutional Council, whose approval of Parliamentary Standing Orders must now be obtained, decided that votes on resolutions were unconstitutional.[2]

The controversy is important because it indicates a possible weakness in the approach to the new institutions of certain of their supporters. It has been stated earlier that the purpose of the Constitution was to create a new relationship between Government and Parliament, closer to that which exists between Government and Opposition in Great Britain and, in the absence of a two-party system, to do so by laying down strict Constitutional rules, limiting the capacity of Parliaments to make the lives of Ministers intolerable, even when they did not go so far as to defeat the Government.

[1] The Assembly later withdrew its provisions for votes following oral questions with debate, after a long argument between Deputies and Government. Provisions for resolutions were retained. The Senate retained both procedures. Resolutions were voted in both Houses, before the procedure was declared unconstitutional. The Senate's case for retaining both procedures was that, since Governments are not responsible to the Senate, and the latter cannot, therefore, use the procedures laid down in article 49, to refuse it the right to criticize would be to reduce its status to that of a purely consultative organ without authority or prestige. This was also the view of the Senate under the Fourth Republic and it was M. Debré himself, as a Senator, who was responsible for the introduction, and extensive use, in the Senate of oral questions with debate. The constitutionality of the procedure was contested in some quarters, but it continued to be used by the Senate throughout the Fourth Republic.

[2] Resolutions are now in order only if they deal with matters concerning the organization of the House itself or if they are decisions to bring someone before the High Court of Justice, or to set up Commissions of inquiry or supervision (v. Règlement de l'Assemblée Nationale, September 1959, article 82).

t has also been pointed out earlier that French Constitutions have ften reacted too far against what they disliked in the previous égime. Both these points may be relevant to the evolution of relaions between Government and Parliament during the Fifth Republic. It is true, as was pointed out in defence of the Government position, that British Members of Parliament do not feel the eed to have a vote following Parliamentary questions. But there is o real analogy between British and French procedure on this point, ecause the party structures and Parliamentary habits of the two ountries are fundamentally different. The fears of those who bjected to a vote on a resolution following oral questions with ebate arose from the possibility that the Government, though it ould not be constitutionally defeated, could, nevertheless, receive minority of the votes cast and so appear to the country to be oing against the will of the Assembly. Such a situation would be nthinkable in the British Parliament, where the Government esigns if it is clear that it cannot count on a majority to see its policy hrough. British practice is not based on mechanical or arithmetical ules, but on political facts.

Some of those who defended the condemned procedures were, a fact, seeking not to weaken Governments, but to strengthen nem, by providing a safety-valve permitting criticisms of the rovernment on specific issues, by Deputies who did not necessarily ant to challenge the Government's right to exist by setting in notion the procedure required for a vote of censure. It may be that ne vital difference between the French and British systems, namely, ne absence in France of either a coherent majority or a coherent pposition, renders necessary certain safety-valves that are not equired in a system which not only has both, but has, in addition, basic unity of Parliamentary habits.[1] An effort to eliminate French

[1] v. for instance, M. Guy Mollet's suggestion that a debate could be followed y a vote on a *Motion d'orientation* (*Le Monde*, 5th June 1959), the *bureau* f the Assembly being authorized to decide whether its formulation was such to make it in order. v. also speech by M. Legaret (*Indépendant*) on the debate f 26th May 1959 on the Standing Orders: 'To permit resolutions to be folwed by a vote is to create an opportunity for an exchange of opinion. A

divisions by acting as if they did not exist may well have the result not of encouraging Deputies to acquire the desired new Parlia mentary habits, but rather that of increasing their ingenuit in exploiting old and familiar ones. It may, however, help to en courage Deputies to make more intelligent use of the Parliamentar question than they have done up to now.

It is possible that the changes in legislative procedure may en counter similar obstacles. Governments now have the constitutiona authority to dominate in legislative debates in the Assembly. The have certain rights that they did not previously possess—the righ to priority for Government Bills in the Parliamentary time-table the right to open the general debate on a Bill in either House, an also the right to propose Government amendments instead c having to resort to undignified subterfuges. This means tha Deputies now hear the case for the Bill before they hear the critic isms of it contained in the report of the relevant Commission and they now debate on the basis of the Government's Bill, instea of on the Bill as amended in Commission.[1] Governments also nov have power to restrict the exercise of certain rights possessed b Deputies. They can object to amendments from the floor, if thes are put forward after the debate has begun—that is, without havin been submitted to the Commission; they may ask the House t decide by a single vote on the whole Bill, or part of it, taking int

refusal to allow them means that Parliament will be forced to reject th budget, or else, as it did in 1924, all Government proposals. It means sub stituting bad temper for frank explanations' (*Le Monde*, 28th May 1959 Cf. too the opinion of M. Brocas (Radical): 'It is essential that Parliamen should be able to express its political opinions by a vote other than a vote c censure.' Even the *rapporteur* of the *Commission du Règlement*, a U.N.I Deputy, expressed the hope that the Government would itself initiate debate on subjects of general interest in order to ensure that the opposition would b able to express its opinion freely, now that resolutions were out of order (*L Monde*, 23rd July 1959).

[1] The debate did not always take place on the basis of the Commission version. Sometimes the Government obtained the assent of the Assembly t a proposal to consider the Government's version.

consideration only their own amendments, or amendments approved by them. If there is disagreement between the two Houses on a Bill, Governments can help to see that their own views prevail. If they are in favour of a Bill they can enable the Assembly to vote it in spite of the Senate's opposition; if they are opposed to it, they can, in effect, back the Senate against the Assembly, by refusing to intervene, thus ensuring that the Bill drops. What they cannot do, of course, is to obtain the passage of a Bill voted by the Senate but rejected by the Assembly.

The Government's control over finance

Under the Fifth Republic, the constitutional right of Deputies or Senators to propose measures involving an increase of expenditure is also severely curtailed. Similar, though less drastic restrictions existed on paper during the previous régime and it remains to be seen whether Governments will, in the future, have more authority than they have had in the past to secure their enforcement in practice. It is perhaps worth while to recall briefly the methods by which the intentions expressed in the 1946 Constitution and in subsequent enactments were frustrated by Deputies, for one thing, because it is by no means certain that some of the same tactics may not be employed in the future, and for another, because they illustrate the point just made, namely, that the rigidities of the 1958 Constitution may lead frustrated Deputies to concentrate on finding ways round the obstacles to indulgence in old habits, instead of on developing new ones more in conformity with the spirit of the new Constitution.

Article 17 of the 1946 Constitution prohibited Deputies and Senators from proposing increased expenditure during budget debates. This provision, as well as those of what were known as *lois des maxima* governing certain aspects of budgetary procedure from 1949 onwards,[1] were evaded mainly in two ways. The Finance

---

[1] The *loi des maxima* was an article inserted at the beginning of finance laws from 1949 onwards, reiterating in somewhat more detail and with more precision the prohibition of article 17 of the Constitution.

Commission was the judge of the admissibility of amendments
finance Bills, and, since it was often at loggerheads with the Gover
ment, frequently took a lenient view of doubtful amendmen
Moreover, a Deputy was in order in proposing an amendment,
its adoption would not involve a *net* increase of expenditure,
other words, if he proposed to curtail expenditure elsewhere 1
an amount equivalent to the increase which the adoption of 1
amendment would involve. This second device proved a godse1
to Deputies anxious to prove that they had their electors' interes
at heart. Their amendments could propose real expenditure a1
theoretical—often highly problematical—economies, or expen
ture to be accepted in principle, but incurred only at some futu
date, which absolved them from the responsibility of suggesti1
how the cost was to be met.

A '*décret organique*' of June 1956 tightened up financial pr
cedure in a number of ways. Among other things, it debarr
members of Parliament from proposing amendments to *any* Bill,
their adoption would result in an increase of expenditure. This 1
duced private members' financial initiative to the *introduction*
Bills, and these, of course, could often be killed in Commission. B
the compensatory device was still used to evade the restrictions a1
members also had other weapons in their armoury.

Since the control of the purse is an essential principle of Parli
mentary government, Parliament could, and still can, refuse
vote supplies. Under the Fourth Republic it could do this in tw
ways, by delaying the vote until certain conditions had been met,
by rejecting the budget altogether. The 1958 Constitution preven
delaying tactics by imposing a time-limit for budgetary debates,
the end of which, if Parliament has not voted on the proposals, t1
Government is authorized to introduce the provisions by decree
Finance Ministers of the Fifth Republic will, therefore, not fi1
themselves in the position occupied by M. Faure at the beginni1
of 1952, when the Assembly had authorized the expenditure pr

---

[1] On the procedure for voting finance Bills *v. supra*, p. 99.

ded for in his budget, but had refused to vote on the articles
oviding for the revenue to meet it.

Parliament's second weapon remains. The threat to reject the
dget altogether, failing certain concessions by the Government,
n still place Ministers of the Fifth Republic in the position occupied
M. Faure in March 1955, when his request for special powers to
ply certain tax reforms by decree was granted only on condition
at he agreed to withdraw a highly unpopular (and highly effective)
ethod of combating tax evasion.

Nor is it certain that Governments can prevent Parliament from
ntinuing to do what it has done in the past—either to interpret a
ovision in such a way as to render it ineffective, or to whittle
wn or defer indefinitely the application of measures agreed to in
inciple, as M. Mendès-France's measures in 1954 to restrict the
ivileges of private distillers and beetroot growers were sabotaged
practice by repeated decisions on the part of Parliament to defer
eir application.[1]

The following three incidents may be indicative of some of the
oblems that Governments may have to face in their attempts to
tablish a new relationship between Government and Assembly in
e field of financial legislation. One of the first measures proposed
a private member in the new Assembly was that of an old Radical
eputy, with forty years' Parliamentary experience behind him,
iose plan to restore certain ex-servicemen's pensions (the sup-
ession of which by the provisional Government was generally un-
pular) included the suggestion that the cost could be met by a
nple transference of the necessary funds from the Ministry of
efence to the Ministry of Pensions! When doubts were expressed
the Finance Commission in July 1959 regarding the possibilities,
der the new Constitution, of Parliamentary amendments to the
overnment's proposals for fiscal reform, the President, M. Paul
ynaud, another veteran Parliamentarian of the Fourth Republic,
d a former Finance Minister as well as a former Prime Minister,
minded members that they still possessed the right of amendment

[1] They had still not been applied in 1959.

'on condition that any diminution of revenue is compensated for]
genuine corresponding increase of revenue'.[1] In the budget d
bates at the end of 1959, the Prime Minister had to yield to pre
sure from the Assembly and agree to a partial restoration
ex-servicemen's pensions in 1960, and full restoration in 196
if the financial circumstances made it possible. Even before t
end of the first Parliamentary session, some of the Gaullist Deputi
were discovering, one of the essential facts of French Parli
mentary life—the influence of the elector on the individual D
puty who is anxious to be re-elected. Whether Governmei
will be able to canalize this influence into channels less disrupti
than those of the past will be one of the most important te
of the ability of the Fifth Republic to avoid falling into the errc
of the Fourth.

Executive weapons against the Assembly

(a) INCOMPATIBILITY. The consequences of the rule of 'incompa
bility' between the functions of Minister and of Deputy have be
discussed so far only in relation to the electoral system.[2] Its inf

[1] The *loi organique* of 2nd January 1959 governing the voting of finar
laws specifically states (article 42) that 'no additional article and no amendm
to a finance Bill is in order unelss its purpose is to suppress or effectively
reduce an item of expenditure'. The wording is almost the same as that
article 58 of the *décret organique* of 19th June 1956.

The difficulty occurs also with Bills other than finance Bills and is mai
one of interpretation. Strictly speaking, most proposals, if adopted, invol
expenditure. M. Pleven pointed out that a resolution (if he had been speaki
a few months later he would have had to say Bill or amendment) asking
Government to ratify the convention on the strengthening of measures
suppress prostitution had been ruled out of order on the ground that
accept the proposal would involve increased expenditure on police. On t
basis, he added, the Finance Commission could reject a resolution proposi
the abolition of the death penalty on the ground that execution would
cheaper than imprisonment (quoted in *Le Monde*, 30th May 1959).

[2] *v. supra*, p. 65.

The Member of Parliament who becomes a Minister must resign his s
within a month. During that month he may not vote. On leaving the Gove
ment ex-Ministers formerly employed in one of the categories of the pub

ce on the relations between Government and Parliament may be
r-reaching. The inclusion of this rule in the Constitution is
nerally attributed to General de Gaulle, whose faith in the effica-
ty of the separation of powers is well known. Its supporters hope
at it will help to increase Governmental stability. They believe that
eputies may hesitate to turn Governments out in the hope of
btaining office for themselves, if the price is giving up their seat in
e Assembly, and that Ministers will obtain a welcome relief from
rty pressure, both in the Assembly and in the constituencies
r which they were elected.

As many of them are Mayors in these constituencies and may
ell be candidates again in the same constituency, the latter hope,
least, is bound to be disappointed. The incompatibility rule has
so other, and more serious disadvantages. If it does, in fact, deter
le Deputies (or Senators) from seeking office, then the quality
Ministers may deteriorate. If the Prime Minister looks outside
e ranks of politicians for his colleagues, as the first Prime Minister
the Fifth Republic did, in the main,[1] then fresh problems are
eated; for instance, that of maintaining the necessary contacts
tween Ministers and public opinion, and that of the possible
terioration in the quality of both Ministers and the Civil Service if
t merely Ministers, but also their private secretariats (*cabinets*),
e to be generally recruited from the higher ranks of the admini-
ration. France is rightly proud of the quality of her higher Civil

rvice incompatible with Ministerial office receive their full salary for a period
six months, unless they find paid employment before then. They are not
owed during that period to take any post as director, or managing director
a nationalized concern, or as legal adviser to such a concern, nor may they
ke any such posts in concerns subsidized by the State, unless they had oc-
pied such a post prior to becoming Ministers.

[1] In the first Government of the Fifth Republic, three important posts were
ld by politicians. They were Finance (M. Pinay), Justice (M. Michelet)
d that of M. Soustelle, whose functions were less important than his per-
nality. The portfolios of foreign affairs, the army, education, industry and
mmerce, public health, housing and the interior were all held by high
vil servants, as was that of Delegate-General for Algeria.

Servants. But if the ranks of these are regularly depleted, the Civil Service's loss will by no means necessarily be the Government gain. Nothing in the conduct of affairs since June 1958 indicates th Civil Servants make particularly good Ministers. Indeed, more th one happening since then has borne out the contention that one the most valuable functions of Ministers is the political one of tellin Civil Servants what the public will not stand. There is also th danger that, after having been indifferent Ministers, Civil Servan may be less good Civil Servants. The problem of the 'politicizatio of the Civil Service could be serious. For either the Minister go back to his original job, in which case he will often be inescapab associated with the policy he has followed as a Minister, or else I will be moved elsewhere in order to avoid this result—to give hi time to *se refaire une virginité administrative*—in which case th quality of the administration may suffer.

The incompatibility rule is criticizable also on the ground that th isolation of Governments from public opinion is bound to I increased if Ministers (whether politicians or technicians) are cut o from contact with opinion in the Assembly. It is true that the Assen bly is itself often accused of being out of touch with public opinio It has traditionally considered itself to be the authentic expressio of popular sovereignty—*le pays légal*, as opposed to *le pays réel*— and, as such, it has been, on the one hand, too sensitive to certa aspects of public opinion, to pressure from local interests and pre sure groups, for instance, and, on the other hand, often insensitiv to general feeling in the country, because it constitutes a 'hou without windows', a closed club, whose political controversies ar values are not appreciated by the average citizen. It is neverthele to the Assembly that Governments remain responsible and it surely preferable that pressure groups should exert their influen there, through the normal channels of Parliamentary group rather than in the semi-secrecy of technocratic *cabinets* or in par meetings outside the Assembly. 'The worst Chamber will alwa be better than the best antechamber.'[1] For, though he ceases to be

[1] G. Morange, op. cit., p. 26.

ember of the Assembly (or of the Senate), the Minister remains a
ember of his party. While Governments have a docile Parlia-
entary majority the disadvantages of 'incompatibility' may not be
lly apparent, though even with a comfortable majority behind
im, M. Debré's inability to handle the Assembly was responsible
r some awkward moments during the first session. If the
overnment ever has to fight for its majority the relations between
inisters and Parliamentary groups could be vital in determining
s fate.[1]

) DISSOLUTION. Nor is the weapon of dissolution, henceforth to be
ed at the discretion of the President of the Republic,[2] likely to
rove an effective substitute for good working relations between
overnment and Assembly. The only example of a dissolution
uring the present century was that of M. Faure in 1955. It was
aused by Parliamentary deadlock over the electoral system. But
e electoral campaign, in so far as it had any dominant theme at all,
as concerned almost wholly with Algeria, on which the dissolved
arliament had had no coherent policy either. The result of the
ection was to produce an Assembly in which the balance of opinion
n both these issues was virtually unchanged.

There is no reason to think that subsequent dissolutions would
e more successful in obtaining from the electorate a clear expres-
on of opinion, for the simple reason that neither French parties
r French elections are organized in such a way as to produce a
ear choice for any coherent policy. The elector votes for a party,
r an electoral label, which often has no national organization be-
nd it and whose relations with neighbouring parties or groups
n vary from constituency to constituency. He has, therefore, no
ossibility of judging the relation between his choice of a candidate
d the complexion of any future Government. This will be a

---

[1] After the municipal elections in 1959, M. Debré announced that he was
eking to strengthen the contacts between the Government and the parties
aking up the parliamentary majority.
[2] v. infra, pp. 140–2, on the President's right to dissolve the Assembly.

I

coalition, whose programme, if it has one, is hammered out b
hard bargaining between parties *after* the election.[1]

A great deal of confusion has been created in French thinkin
about dissolution by fallacious comparisons with British practic
During the last years of the Fourth Republic a number of politician
and political scientists put forward proposals for a dissolutio
sometimes automatic, sometimes semi-automatic, or at the discre
tion of the Prime Minister. In French writings on dissolution, th
usual justification for it is the need for the Government to resolv
a conflict with the Assembly by appealing to the nation, or b
threatening to do so, which may in itself be sufficient to brin
Deputies to heel. Now this situation is in no way comparable t
any conceivable one in which a British Government might ask for
dissolution. As has already been pointed out, the system of Cabin
Government in a two-party system normally rules out a confli
between Government and Parliament. A dissolution would rarel
constitute a threat to the Opposition; since the Government
already in power, it would usually stand to lose more than th
Opposition. Nor is there any justification for assuming that
threat of dissolution might bring recalcitrant individual members t
heel. They might all be holders of safe seats.

The truth is that in a multi-party system, as it exists in Franc
where parties are not in the habit of forming coalitions to fig
elections on national programmes that are intended to be Gover
mental programmes, where the line between Government an
Opposition is never wholly clear, and sometimes both unclear an
inconsistent, a dissolution is bound to be a leap in the dark.
may thus become an instrument of political manoeuvre. Before th
Fifth Republic was six months old, certain Deputies were beginnin
to calculate the party advantages that might be derived from see
ing to create the circumstances in which the President mig
dissolve the Assembly. It would seem, therefore, that dissolutio

[1] An election in which there was one dominating theme, say Algeri
might constitute an exception to the general rule.

cannot be counted on to strengthen a Government against the Assembly.[1]

(c) THE REFERENDUM. The objections to a dissolution as a means of strengthening the Government are not wholly applicable to a referendum. In the first place, the Prime Minister has the initiative: the President cannot decide on a referendum except at his request, though he may refuse the request. In the second place, it is easier for the electorate to give a clear answer to a specific question than it is for it to pronounce on the Government's policy as a whole. On the other hand, the use of the referendum is limited to three types of measure—those concerning the organization of the public authorities, approving an agreement with the Community, or authorizing ratification of a Treaty which would affect the functioning of institutions. The results of referenda have, moreover, usually revealed a strong conservative tendency on the part of electorates, and the Government might hesitate to use what must, in the nature of the case, be a two-edged weapon, since its results are difficult to calculate. It might conceivably strengthen a Government's hand in specific cases where there was reason to believe that the Government was more in touch with public opinion than the Assembly, where, for instance, a Government was introducing a measure that it expected Parliament to turn down; or as a means of escape, if pressure by the Assembly forced it to introduce a Bill that it did not really want. It could help Parliament as against the Government only if Deputies wanted to hand over the responsibility for a particular measure to the electorate.[2]

[1] General de Gaulle hinted at the beginning of the Parliament at a possible resort to dissolution, if the Government were defeated, and M. Debré, at one moment, threatened to appeal to the country to settle the conflict over oral questions with debate. In July 1959 a right-wing Deputy was speculating on the advantages to his party of an early dissolution, in view of the Constitutional rule that a second one cannot be held until a year has elapsed.

[2] It is usually considered that the authors of the Constitution had in mind an issue such as that presented by the E.D.C. treaty, where both Government and Assembly were divided. The Government of the day might well have

Government and President

In one respect, Governments of the Fifth Republic may be weaker than their predecessors. It is clear from what has just been said that, where President and Prime Minister are not agreed, the President can constitutionally, in certain circumstances, go against the advice of the Prime Minister. The latter could then be caught between two fires, and be faced with two conflicts where his predecessors had only one. Whether this happens or not is a matter that will be decided by the working relationship that is established between the Prime Minister and the President, and by the position that the Presidency comes to occupy under the Fifth Republic.

One of the most controversial questions raised by the pseudo- or semi-presidential system of government of the Fifth Republic is precisely that of the authority and prestige that Governments can normally expect to enjoy. Conclusions must remain for some time speculative, but, so far, three different views have emerged. According to one (a Gaullist view), Senate, President and Prime Minister will form 'a single bloc, the granite mass the driving force and the principle of stability of the Fifth Republic'.[1] According to some opponents of the régime, there is likely to be a return to the traditional relations between President and Prime Minister, the powers now exercised by the President reverting to the Prime Minister. A third view is that, at least until General de Gaulle's Presidency comes to an end, the Prime Minister will be a mouthpiece of the President, who will be the effective head of the Government as well as the head of the State. So far, the facts have certainly justified the third of these views.

preferred not to assume the responsibility for what was a difficult decision and one that, in the end, it never wholeheartedly took. A number of Deputies, too, would not have objected to handing over responsibility to the electorate.

[1] Marcel Prélot, *Pour comprendre la nouvelle Constitution* (*Editions Le Centurion*, 1958), p. 54.

CHAPTER VIII

The Presidency

The Presidential tradition and General de Gaulle

The 16 Presidents of the Third and Fourth Republics have a certain family resemblance, because most of them were chosen to conform to a pattern. French members of Parliament have preferred to elect as President an elder statesman, generally respected by his fellow-members of Parliament, but neither an outstanding political leader nor a man of strong or extreme party views. All 16 had been members of, and ten had been President of, one or other of the two Houses of Parliament. All but four were over 60 and two were over 70.

There are naturally a few exceptions to the general rule. Both Poincaré and Millerand had been Prime Ministers and M. Auriol had been not merely a prominent pre-war political leader, but was also the first and only Socialist to become President of the Republic. At the other extreme, one or two came near to possessing the qualifications recommended by Clemenceau, who advised his colleagues to 'vote for the most stupid', or those objected to by M. Herriot, when he accused the authors of the 1946 Constitution of trying to turn the President into a puppet. At the best, the qualities of Republican Presidents have been the kind of personal integrity and political wisdom possessed by M. Auriol, who did much to build up the prestige of the office in the early days of the Fourth Republic, or by his successor, M. Coty, who had the even more difficult task of helping to make possible a peaceful and legal transition to the Fifth.

Republican Presidents have not, as a rule, enjoyed peaceful periods of office. Some would have liked to play a more active rôle than the one allotted to them and were forced to choose one of the alternatives put before Marshal MacMahon—to give in or to get out (*se soumettre ou se démettre*). Indeed, three were forced to resign (though one of them had already by then been re-elected for a second term), two were murdered, one died in office, two resigned because of the collapse of the régime (though one had been re-elected for a second term) and three resigned for various reasons before the completion of their period of office. Only five completed their period of office normally.

The first President of the Fifth Republic is an exception to most of the rules. He is the first regular-army officer to become President since Marshal MacMahon did so in 1873. He is the first President not to have been a member of Parliament. He was from 1940 to 1946 the acknowledged leader of the nation, first in exile and then at the head of the provisional Government, and he was, from 1947 to 1953, an outstanding political leader of the opposition to both the Constitution and the policies of the Fourth Republic. In normal circumstances, neither his personality nor his political opinions would have been considered by the majority of Frenchmen as recommendations for the post of President. Nor was the post one that would have recommended itself to him. The office of President has therefore, undergone a sea-change, which General de Gaulle was largely instrumental in bringing about. One result is that, for the first time since 1924, the President has become a subject of political controversy. The office, too, is under criticism. Among the many Articles of the new Constitution that have been adversely commented on, those governing the functions of the President have been the most severely and the most generally criticized.

In one fundamentally important respect, both the new conception of the office and its first holder are, on paper at least, in line with both Republican and Presidential traditions. The Constitution provides for a President who is to be Head of the State, but who in normal circumstances is not head of the Government. The functions of directing the Government and of determining its policy are specifically entrusted by the Constitution to the Prime Minister

(Article 20). A President can, and should, therefore, take a back seat, just as his predecessors did. General de Gaulle has indubitably occupied the driving seat in some fields and has intervened in most, but the circumstances in which he came to power make it impossible to predict the evolution or the office in normal conditions.

The Presidential election

Presidents of the Fifth Republic are elected for seven years and presumably are indefinitely re-eligible, since the Constitution does not, as the 1946 Constitution did, specifically limit the number of terms of office. No qualifications for the office are mentioned either, the sole disqualification laid down in the 1946 Constitution—membership of a former reigning family of France—having been dropped. Election is by two ballots, unless a candidate obtains an absolute majority of the votes cast at the first. A simple majority only is required at the second. The Presidential electors include, along with Deputies and Senators, who elected the President under the two preceding régimes, an overwhelming majority of representatives of local authorities. With three exceptions, the Presidential electoral college is the same as that for the Senate. These exceptions are: (i) the inclusion of representatives of both the legislative and local Assemblies of the member-States of the Community,[1] since the President of the Republic is also *ex-officio* President of the Community; (ii) the choice as electors, in villages of up to 9,000 inhabitants, of Mayors and Councillors, instead of special delegates[2]

---

[1] On the proportion of electors from the member-States, *v. infra*, p. 159n. 1.

[2] For villages of up to 9,000 representatives are as follows:

Up to 1,000, the Mayor.

1,000–2,000: the Mayor and the first assistant Mayor.

2,001–2,500: the Mayor and the first assistant Mayor, and the Municipal Councillor with the highest number of votes at the previous Municipal election.

2,501–3,000: the Mayor and the first two assistants.

3,001–6,000: the Mayor and the first two assistants and three Municipal Councillors with the highest number of votes.

6,001–9,000: the Mayor and the first two assistants and six Municipal Councillors with the highest number of votes.

elected by the Municipal Council; and (iii) a slightly less spectacular overweighting of the representation of small villages. The representation of towns and villages with over 9,000 inhabitants is on exactly the same basis as for the Senatorial college.

The system is obviously open to criticisms similar to those made of the Senatorial college. In spite of the slightly different composition, the representatives of villages with under 1,500 inhabitants still constitute a clear majority (51 per cent, as against 53 per cent). In 1958, Paris, with a population of about 2,800,000, had 2,910 Presidential electors. According to Professor Duverger, communes with under 300 inhabitants, whose combined populations were only 2,850,000, had 16,312 electors. The President is, in reality elected by village Mayors.

This system has been defended by, among others, M. Debré whose argument was that France is a country of small villages. It has also been defended on the rather weak ground that since both the previous system and election by universal suffrage had to be ruled out—the former as affording the President insufficient prestige (the 13 ballots required for the election of M. Coty in 1953 certainly did not provide a dignified spectacle) and the latter too much— there was really no alternative. The disproportionality was explained away on the ground that small *communes* had a right to their say, and that giving them a less disproportionate say would have involved the special election of delegates, with the consequent risk of 'politicization'. It has been criticized, in particular by M. Duverger, on the ground that, like the Senatorial electoral system, it is an effort to restore a *régime des notables*, though whether, in this day and age, French village Mayors can still be legitimately regarded as 'notabilities' in the old sense is debatable. In the larger towns and in some villages, local government elections are largely political, and even in the villages, the rôle of the *curé* and the *château* is not what it was. The Mayor is certainly an important personage and a genuine representative. But one must distinguish 'between those

---

[1] The 1958 Presidential electorate numbered 81,512, of whom 76,310 represented metropolitan France. The 1959 Senatorial College numbered 108,266

who are notabilities by virtue of their election and those who are elected because they are notabilities'.[1]

There are at least two serious objections to the system. One is that, if there are more than two or three candidates, the President may be elected on a minority vote. This would defeat the ostensible purpose of the system, which is to make the President, at one and the same time, a representative of the nation, and one who cannot legitimately claim to be *as* representative as those chosen by universal suffrage. Provision is made for only two ballots. Electors vote in the administrative centre for the *département* (in the case of the electors of the States of the Community, in their own countries). It is likely to be extremely difficult for any agreement to be reached between electors between the two ballots in order to prevent a candidate from being elected on the second ballot by a minority vote.[2] Even under the previous system, when under 1,000 electors were all under one roof and an unlimited number of ballots could be held until a candidate obtained an absolute majority, agreement on a candidate was often very difficult.

The second serious objection to the system is that it is more difficult to change than that governing elections to the Assembly or to the Senate, for unlike the previous Presidential electoral system, that of the Fifth Republic has been included in the Constitution.[3]

The supervision of Presidential elections, including the investigation of alleged irregularities, is entrusted to the Constitutional Council, which carries out the final count (in public) in Paris and announces the results. In case of a Presidential vacancy, the President of the Senate replaces the President until elections can be held.

[1] Jean Rivero, *Regards sur les Institutions de la Ve République* (*Recueil Dalloz Hebdomadaire*, 12th November, 1958, p. 263).

[2] The second ballot is held a week after the first. No new candidate may stand at the second ballot unless presented by two candidates who agree to stand down for him (organic law of 7th November 1958).

[3] The only exceptions to the normal procedure of Constitutional revision would be an increase in the electorate of the member-States under article 6 or a heavy reduction in the number of *communes*.

Traditional Presidential functions

A great many of the functions of the President are, in fact, those traditionally carried out by Republican Presidents. The President appoints the Prime Minister and accepts his resignation. He appoints and dismisses members of the Government, at the request of the Prime Minister, presides at meetings of the Council of Ministers, of Councils and Committees of National Defence and of the Supreme Council of the Judiciary. He negotiates and ratifies treaties, accredits Ambassadors, appoints to some civil and military posts. He signs decrees in the Council of Ministers, promulgates laws (having the right to insist on a second reading by Parliament). He has the right of pardon.

In exercising these mainly formal functions, the President is, like his predecessors, acting with the concurrence, and on the initiative, of the Prime Minister, whose counter-signature, together with that of any other relevant Ministers, is necessary before he can act. The one exception is, of course, his appointment of the Prime Minister, for which, in the nature of the case, the resigning Government cannot take responsibility.

In a few respects, the Constitution gives the President of the Fifth Republic, even where these functions are concerned, a little more elbow room than his predecessors have had, but it is too soon to estimate the extent of real Presidential power that the changes will normally involve. For instance, the President now 'negotiates' Treaties (article 52), whereas under the previous Constitution he was merely 'kept informed' of the negotiations.[1] The list of offices to which he has the right of appointment is far longer than that contained in the 1946 Constitution. The President nominates the Prime Minister and the members of the Government proposed to him by the Prime Minister, without having to go through the intermediate stage of *désignation*.[2] In one respect, he seems to have somewhat less opportunity of independent action. To exercise the

[1] But *v. infra*, pp. 146–7.   [2] *v. supra*, p. 115n. 1, on *désignation*.

ight of pardon he now requires a counter-signature, whereas the previous Constitution did not mention this requirement.[1]

Like his predecessors under the Third and Fourth Republics, the President is politically irresponsible for acts carried out by him in pursuance of his functions, except in the case of high treason, for which he can be tried before the High Court of Justice.[2] This provision is comprehensible in the case of a President who presides but does not govern, but less so in that of a President of the Fifth Republic who, even in normal circumstances, can exercise some degree of real power, and who, in an emergency, has the right to exercise unlimited power.

The concept of the arbitrator

The new powers possessed in normal circumstances by Presidents of the Fifth Republic really fall into two categories. First, the President can make a certain number of appointments without a counter-signature. It may, of course, be that Presidents will follow precedents in these cases and that the element of personal choice will be small, or in any case, that the choice will not be likely to give the President any significant additional powers. These are really powers exercised by virtue of the President's function, described in article 5, as guardian of the Constitution:

> The President of the Republic sees that the Constitution is respected, ensures by his arbitration the regular functioning of the organs of government and the continuity of the State.

> He is the protector (*le garant*) of national independence, of territorial integrity, and of respect for agreements within the Community and for Treaties.

[1] It is worth remembering that the first President of the Fourth Republic, M. Auriol, though he sought advice on the matter of pardons, did not have a counter-signature. The constitutionality of this procedure was questioned by some.

[2] *v. supra*, p. 49.

This concept, in itself, constitutes no break with Presidential tradition, though General de Gaulle interprets it very differently from the way in which his predecessors would have done. M. Auriol certainly considered that one of his functions was to ensure respect for the Constitution.[1] And, according to accounts, it was M. Coty who outlined to General de Gaulle the precise procedure which would reconcile his own conditions with constitutional requirements.

The President's right to submit a treaty before ratification, or a law before promulgation, to the Constitutional Council, on the ground that it appears to be unconstitutional (articles 54 and 61) and his right to appoint three of the nine members of the Constitutional Council (article 56) seem clearly to be aspects of this function, differing only from other traditional Presidential functions in that there is no counter-signature.

General de Gaulle sees as falling within the scope of his functions as an arbitrator a second category of Presidential powers, which might be described as the right either to appeal or to refuse to appeal to the nation. The President has the right to have messages read in both Houses (article 18). He may decide, either to accede to, or to refuse, a request submitted to him by the Prime Minister (during Parliamentary sessions) or by the two Houses conjointly, for a referendum on a Government Bill dealing with the organization of the public authorities, approving a Community agreement, or authorizing the ratification of a treaty which affects the functioning of institutions (article 11). And he may decide, after consulting the Prime Minister and the Presidents of the two Houses, to dissolve the National Assembly (article 12).

None of these rights enables the President to intervene directly in the processes of government. They are optional and exceptional by their nature. The referendum can be used only in the specific cases mentioned and the right of dissolution cannot be used more

---

[1] v. for instance, his speech of 15th November 1951: 'As I see my function, it is to defend the State, its Constitution, its institutions and also the permanent interests of France that this State represents.'

han once a year, since the Constitution prohibits a further dis-
olution within a year following a previous one.[1] Both referendum
nd dissolution explicitly hand over the right of decision to the
lectorate. Nevertheless, the choice of the circumstances in which
hese instruments are used could be a political choice.

While General de Gaulle remains in office, his interpretation of
hese powers might well go unchallenged, What has created dis-
juiet is the constitutionalization of powers acceptable to Republican
radition only in abnormal circumstances, and for a limited time.

There are several ways in which the use of these three powers
ould involve a President in political controversy. It was evident,
or instance, in May 1958, that M. Coty's Presidential message,
hreatening to resign if Parliament refused to accept General de
Gaulle's candidature as Prime Minister, had a considerable influ-
nce on Deputies. This message was, of course, counter-signed by
he Prime Minister, in conformity with the requirements of the 1946
Constitution. It is easy to imagine how, in a similarly tense situation,
 President free to address both Houses on his own initiative and to
xpress his own opinion rather than that of the Government might
e able to influence the course of events. A Presidential decision to
issolve the Assembly could, in certain circumstances, enable a
President to get rid of a Prime Minister, though the Constitution
ives him no direct right to do this. For instance, in a case of con-
ict between President and Prime Minister, a well-timed dissolution
ould result in the return of an Assembly favourable to the Pre-
ident's point of veiw, and so force the Government to resign. In
he same circumstances, an ill-judged dissolution could place a
President in the situation of President MacMahon in 1877, and so
rce the President to resign.

On the other hand, a misjudged dissolution, by which a President
ied, and failed, to produce an Assembly more amenable to the
Government's point of view, must surely bring the President into

[1] If the President of the Senate is called on to act as *interim* President, he
nnot use the powers of the President in relation to the referendum and the
issolution.

disrepute along with the Government. For, by voting against a
Government supported by the President, the electorate would, in
effect, be voting against the President too.

The Presidential right to refuse a request for a referendum is the
right to decide not to submit to the electorate an issue that either the
Government or Parliament considers ought to be so submitted.
In deciding to exercise the right, a President would, therefore,
either be siding with Parliament against the Government or with
the Government against Parliament. In either case his position as
an arbitrator would be weakened.

These examples assume that the Fifth Republic will remain a
Parliamentary system. If it becomes, in reality, a semi-Presidential
system, in which the President and not the Prime Minister is the
effective head of the Government, then new Parliamentary and
Governmental habits may be formed making possible personal decisions of the kind envisaged. But failing such changes in French
habits, to be an 'arbitrator', a President must not only be impartial,
he must be *seen* to be impartial.

Emergency powers

The article of the Constitution which aroused more criticism than
all the others put together is that defining the President's power in
abnormal circumstances. It is worth while, therefore, quoting its
provisions in full.

> In a situation in which there is an immediate and serious threat
> to Republican institutions, national independence, territorial
> integrity or the application of international agreements, and in
> which the regular functioning of the constitutional organs of
> government is interrupted, the President of the Republic, after
> officially consulting the Prime Minister, the Presidents of the
> Assemblies and the Constitutional Council, takes the measures
> called for by the circumstances.
>
> He informs the nation by a message.
>
> These measures, on which the Constitutional Council is to be

consulted, must be inspired by the will to enable the organs of government to fulfil their mission with the minimum of delay. Parliament meets as of right. The National Assembly cannot be dissolved while the emergency powers are in force.

In General de Gaulle's mind, the intention of this article was both precise and limited. It was intended to be used solely as a reserve power, in the event of a national disaster such as the defeat of 1940, or to enable the necessary instructions to be given if the political and administrative organs were to be disorganized by, say, an atomic war. The principle of the need to assure the continuity of the State has not been contested. What has been generally contested, outside Gaullist circles, is that the method chosen would achieve its purpose. Even if M. Lebrun had possessed these powers in 1940, the situation would have been unchanged. It was not, in actual fact, the weakness of Presidential authority that was responsible for the capitulation and for the handing over of political powers to Marshal Pétain, but a regular vote of the two Houses of Parliament.

The fundamental objection raised by critics of the article is that its provisions could be deliberately abused by a President seeking personal power, and could even serve as technically legal cover for a *coup d'état*. The President alone is entitled to decide when an emergency, as defined by the Constitution, exists, and what measures should be taken. His obligations are merely to *consult* the Presidents of the two Houses and the Constitutional Council and to *inform* the nation. Neither the provision that Parliament meets as of right and cannot be dissolved during the emergency, nor that requiring the Constitutional Council to publish its opinions regard-the existence of an emergency, with reasons, provides any real safeguard against Presidential unconstitutionality, since the President has the right to assume full powers. Supporters of the Constitution dismiss these objections, on the ground that the measures are designed to deal with some remote and improbable contingency, for which, in any case, detailed provisions would be impossible.[1]

[1] Two other objections to the article are, first, that its provisions are likely to be unenforceable. In the circumstances postulated, it is very probable that

The imponderables and the 'style' of General de Gaulle

If these fears are not realized, is the Presidential office under the Fifth Republic likely to be very different from what it was under the previous régime? The traditional functions are very much the same and are largely theoretical; the most important of the new powers are intended for use either in exceptional or in highly abnormal circumstances, which may never occur; the second President of the Fifth Republic may, as has been suggested, conform to the traditional pattern, since, in normal circumstances, the composition of the electoral college might be expected to encourage the choice of the conventional, middle-of-the-road, moderate Conservatives who constituted the majority of the Presidents of the Third Republic.

Very little can yet be said about the office, as such, because both the personality of the first President and the circumstances in which he was elected were exceptional. General de Gaulle's prestige is unprecedented and extends throughout the Community. The early days of his term of office not only constituted a time of crisis, but coincided also with the setting up of the Community overseas, with the election at home of a National Assembly unique in French history, and with the choice as first Prime Minister of the Fifth Republic of a man who was both inexperienced in that office and a faithful and long-standing follower of the President. The conditions governing the relations between the first President,

the Constitutional Council and Parliament would be unable to meet. The requirement to consult imposes delay, while one justification of the President's powers is the need for speed.

The second objection is that the article, like so many others, is both obscure and ambiguous and leaves a great many essential questions unanswered. For instance, if the Constitutional Council, or Parliament could not meet, would the President be able constitutionally to apply the provisions of the article? Have the President's powers any limits? Can he, for example, suspend the the application of any parts of the Constitution? Is he the sole judge of the end as well as of the beginning of the emergency? If Parliament does succeed in meeting has it any powers or any rights? For example, is the President under any obligation to inform Parliament of what he is doing?

Government and Assembly, therefore, offer no reliable guidance to the relations that may exist between another President, other Prime Ministers and a different Assembly facing different political problems.

Inevitably, General de Gaulle has played a more active and personal rôle than might be expected of a President holding office in normal circumstances. To take one example, his wide powers of personal decision as President of the Community could be explained either by positive distrust of the intentions of the Parliamentary majority, or perhaps of French Colonial administrators, or by positive confidence in his own capacity to start the new experiment off on the right foot. The future evolution of the Community can involve great changes in the Presidential rôle—all the more so in that the institutions of the Community can be adapted without the need for constitutional revision.

The general assumption that the President and not the Prime Minister is the real source of power in the Fifth Republic is based, not on the nature of the Presidential functions as defined by the Constitution, but on imponderables related to personalities and to the problems of the first year of the régime, as well as on General de Gaulle's own interpretation of his rôle—on what has come to be known as 'the style' of the General. This can perhaps be summed up as consisting of four main elements. The first is a certain conception of the dignity of the office, a belief in the value of Presidential pomp and ceremony, as instanced by the celebrations of 14th July, as a demonstration to the public that France has a leader, that the State exists, to use his own words. The second is a positive, and a very personal interpretation of his function as an arbitrator in his relations with the Government. This sometimes seems to amount to casting Ministers as executants of a policy whose general principles were either determined by him, or deduced by him as expressing the 'general will' in meetings of the Council of Ministers. In other words, he sometimes seemed to 'formulate and notify' decisions of the Council of Ministers, as well as those of the Executive Council of the Community. He has increased the prestige of the

K

Council of Ministers, at meetings of which he presides, reducing the Cabinet Council, presided over by the Prime Minister, to little more than a preparatory organ. Under General de Gaulle's Presidency, the real decisions have not merely been ratified, but often actually taken in the Council of Ministers. Some decisions have clearly been not merely his, but have not even been fully communicated to the Council of Ministers. The important declaration of 16th September 1959 on France's Algerian policy was made by General de Gaulle in person, only a 'general outline' of what he was to say having been communicated to the Council of Ministers. This led one speaker in the Assembly debate the following month to claim that the Fifth Republic had already been replaced by the Sixth.

M. Auriol had, as has been said, a positive view of his functions as an arbitrator, which he described as *une magistrature morale*. At times he intervened very positively during Government crises and in matters affecting the French Union. But there is a world of difference between the two approaches. M. Auriol permitted himself to criticize the conduct of Deputies only when he was driven to exasperation by prolonged Governmental crises. He would never have delivered the kind of advance warning delivered in January 1959 by General de Gaulle, both to the Government and Parliament. On the formation of the new Government, General de Gaulle remarked: 'Gentlemen, your Government will last for the the duration of this Parliament. There will be no other.' And in his first Presidential message to Parliament he warned Deputies that the consequences of indulging in sectional quarrels instead of identifying themselves with the national interest would be a fresh institutional crisis.

The third manifestation of the President's 'style' is in foreign affairs. The articles of the Constitution which authorize the President to 'negotiate and ratify' treaties and to be informed of the negotiation of agreements not requiring ratification do not, on the face of it, seem to permit of an interpretation which would include such acts as the press Conference of 23rd March 1959 (in itself a quite unprecedented step for a President of the Republic), in which he outlined policy and answered questions, even stating that he would himself attend a 'Summit' Conference—*un aréopage*, as he called it—though this was to be a meeting of heads of Governments, not of States. The negotiations with Chancellor Adenauer and President Eisenhower, the meeting with the Italian Prime Minister, the letter of September 1958 on France's position in N.A.T.O., and other similar activities all show that the effective control of foreign policy is in the hands of the President.

Fourthly, in his visits to Overseas territories, in meetings of the organs of the Community, and by provisions for the participation of representatives of the Community in Republican ceremonies, General de Gaulle has carried into Community affairs the same 'style' that he has given to ceremony at home.

That this 'style' at first helped to improve French morale is undeniable. That it enabled the Community to make a good start is highly probable. Its effects on France's foreign relations were more problematical. Its importance in helping to determine the permanent characteristics of the Presidency must remain for some time wholly a matter of conjecture.

CHAPTER IX

Overseas France and the Community

The background

At the outbreak of the second world war, French overseas possessions occupied almost twice the area covered by British territories overseas (over $4\frac{1}{2}$ million, as against $2\frac{1}{2}$ million square miles). Though French colonialism goes back to the seventeenth century, the period of greatest expansion was during the 65 years of the Third Republic, which saw the addition of the territories of West and Equatorial Africa, Madagascar, the establishment of French Protectorates in Indo-China, Morocco and Tunisia, and the administration under French mandate of Syria, the Lebanon, French Togoland and the Cameroons.

Relations between France and her overseas territories have varied a good deal throughout the past century, but French colonial administration has always been characterized by two tendencies. The first was the tendency to assimilate the administration of dependent territories to that of the mother country—which, in a centralized country like France, meant government from Paris. This was the system characteristic of French rule in Algeria and, from 1946 onwards, in the four 'old Colonies' of Guadeloupe, Martinique, Réunion and Guyana, whose association with France goes back to the eighteenth century. The second was the tendency towards 'association', which developed from the end of the nineteenth century, mainly under the influence of great colonial administrators such as Gallieni and Lyautey, in the North African and far-Eastern Protectorates. These retained their national status and their existing institutions, on to which the *cadres* of French colonial bureaucracy were grafted. The two administrations thus existed side by side. The Protectorates had their own flag, currency, and system of legislation, but the final say in all important decisions lay with the French administration, headed by the High Commissioner, Governor-General, or Resident-General, who represented the French Government.

Both these tendencies continued to co-exist, often uneasily, during the Fourth Republic, which endeavoured to substitute for the concept of Empire that of a 'Union'. The Governments of post-war France were, at first, predominantly left-wing, and favourable in principle to nationalist aspirations. They therefore sought a new approach to colonialism based on free co-operation and real association.

The Fourth Republic and the French Union

The French Union, set up by the 1946 Constitution, differed from the pre-war Empire in three main ways. First, a new concept of citizenship was introduced, which promised to all members the individual rights guaranteed by the Constitution, including the right to be represented in the French Parliament. Voting rights were rapidly extended, so that not only did all territories henceforth elect one or more representatives to both the French Assembly and the Council of the Republic, or Senate, but discrimination between European and assimilated citizens on the one hand and natives on the other were progressively abolished. From 1956 onwards, the double electoral roll survived only in Algeria, and it was suppressed there by the *loi-cadre* of February 1958; women as well as men were enfranchized (though Moslem women did not, in fact, vote until after the collapse of the Fourth Republic), and the number of electors rose from $3\frac{1}{2}$ million in the 1946 election to almost 10 millions in that of 1956. The Third Republic had, it is true, provided for some degree of overseas representation in the French Parliament, but this was limited only to the minority then enjoying French citizenship—which meant, in effect, to Europeans and a few assimilated natives, except in Senegal and the 'old Colonies', which enjoyed universal suffrage. Whereas during the Third Republic, 19 Deputies represented Algeria, the 'old Colonies', Senegal and the Indian enclaves, and seven Senators Algeria and the 'old Colonies', Parliaments of the Fourth Republic included 83 Deputies and 74 Senators representing Algeria and 18 overseas Territories.[1] In other words, nearly one Deputy in seven and one Senator in four represented an overseas constituency.

The second important change introduced by the establishment of the French Union was the creation of a new relationship between France and the former Protectorates, renamed Associated States. Their inhabitants were not, of course, French citizens and so had no Parliamentary representation. They were to be represented in two new advisory Assemblies, one, the Assembly of the Union, to include elected representatives from all overseas Territories, sitting alongside equal numbers chosen by the French Parliament to represent France; the other, the High Council of the Union, to include only representatives of the Associated States and France. These provisions were never fully carried out, and this part of the experiment constituted by the creation of the Union must be considered a failure. Morocco and Tunisia never agreed to join the Union; by 1949, the three Indo-Chinese States were well on the way to independence; by 1956, all five of the intended Associated States were independent. The idea of association between France and former French dependent territories survives, however, in the attempts to define the 'interdependence' of France and the newly independent States of Morocco and Tunisia, and in the provisions of the 1958 Constitution for the 'association' of France with other countries, which could include former dependent territories (article 88).

The third important achievement of the French Union was the

---

[1] The number had originally been 20, but was reduced to 18 before the end of the Fourth Republic, since Indo-China absorbed the former colony of Cochin-China, and the Indian Establishments decided to become part of India. Three of the 74 Senators represented French citizens living abroad, that is, not in French possessions.

attempt to provide for some degree of limited autonomy in the former Colonies, renamed Overseas Territories. Algeria, too, was accorded, by the Statute of 1947, a special status which included some autonomy, particularly financial. But these provisions remained within the general assimilative framework of Algerian administration. Their purpose was to provide for some degree of decentralization and to enable Moslems to participate more fully in the work of administration.

The reforms in the Overseas Territories began as little more than attempts to provide for some native participation in elected local Assemblies. But the growth of nationalism throughout Africa, the loss to France of Indo-China in 1954, the enforced grant of independence to Morocco and Tunisia, and the outbreak of a nationalist rebellion in Algeria at the end of 1954, combined to bring home to French Governments the need to replace the traditional concepts of French colonial rule by others more in tune with the times. The result was the 'outline-law' (*loi-cadre*) of 1956, which provided that all Overseas Territories should have embryo Parliaments, elected by universal suffrage, and a limited degree of self-government exercised through Governmental Councils, headed by a President who soon became, within the sphere of local competence, in effect a Prime Minister.

The application of this outline-law was, undoubtedly, one of the most important achievements of the Fourth Republic and may well have made possible the peaceful evolution of the territories of 'black Africa' within a Franco-African Community, eventually moving towards independence. It consisted essentially of four reforms: (i) the establishment of Governmental Councils elected by the Territorial Assemblies and, though not *de jure* responsible, inevitably bound to become *de facto* responsible to the popularly elected body; (ii) the extension of the powers of Territorial Assemblies in matters of predominantly local concern; (iii) provisions for the africanization of the administration,[1] and (iv) universal suffrage

[1] It was intended that about 50 per cent of the students of the *Ecole Nationale d'Administration* should come from the Overseas Territories.

and the abolition of the double electoral college in the few Territories (Madagascar and Equatorial Africa) in which it still existed.

This meant the end of the tradition of direct French rule, except
for the reserved subjects—admittedly constituting an important
list. France remained responsible for the essential services of foreign
affairs, defence, justice, the maintenance of individual liberties,
communications, finance and foreign exchange and higher education—in all some 32 different services, at the head of which was the
Head of the Territory and President of the Governmental Council,
who was a French official responsible to the relevant Ministry in
Paris.

This reform did not go far enough to satisfy all native leaders,
some of whom, by 1956, were already demanding wider powers and
responsible Governments. But it did represent an immediate advance,
and left the way open for further advance by way of decrees, without involving a revision of the Constitution, which was by then
politically impossible. It was particularly important in that it
represented a new French approach to the problem of colonial
rule.

Why the French Union did not succeed

The colonial problem was peculiarly acute for post-war France
for several reasons. For one thing, the French Empire had consisted
almost exclusively of predominantly coloured populations, both
economically and politically backward, and so the development of
nationalism came later than in British possessions.

It came at a time when France had gone through four years of
defeat and occupation. She was, therefore, suffering from an acute
shortage of the resources, both human and material, needed for the
development of her Overseas Territories. In the circumstances the
degree of financial, technical and economic aid provided for overseas
development was remarkable, when it is remembered how much
reconstruction and modernization was needed at home. For another
thing, nationalism, when it came, found French Governments
politically as well as economically unprepared. Their colonial

traditions had not included provisions either for independence or for anything like Dominion status and, whether based on the principles of assimilation or of association, the administrative systems of French overseas possessions had been characterized by political as well as economic paternalism. In the three North African territories, the existence of large European populations had meant that administrative *cadres* were overwhelmingly European. The European element was correspondingly predominant in the economic field and constituted a powerful political lobby, particularly in the case of Algeria, most of whose million and a quarter Europeans were determined to remain French citizens, and many of whose $8\frac{1}{2}$ million Moslems had every interest in remaining French, since from 300,000 to 400,000 of them were able to find employment only in France. In the African territories South of the Sahara, in spite of the rapid progress from 1956 onwards, African nationalist aspirations soon outran the economic, administrative and political capacities of these politically and economically backward territories. With the exception of Morocco, all French overseas possessions had close economic links with France. Some were dependent for their survival on trade with France; they provided France with a protected market for her exports; they relied on French capital, technicians, teachers, doctors, administrators to run their administrative as well as their economic machine.

Added to these difficulties, there were those caused by the political divisions of post-war France, which meant that, again and again, decisions were deferred until too late. Overdue reforms were out of date before they became law and colonial administrators, left without a lead from Paris, were too often out of sympathy with native nationalist movements and aspirations.

The result of all these difficulties was that successive French Governments failed to agree on the revision of the articles of the Constitution dealing with overseas France, although there was general agreement from 1955 onwards on the need for such revision. When the Fourth Republic collapsed in May 1958, it was clear that the new Constitution would have to face the challenge of African nationalism and that the concept of the French Union was no longer adequate.

The new concept of 'the Community'

The constitution of the Fifth Republic replaces the concept of the French Union by that of 'the Community', a new term which remains undefined, except for the statements that it is 'based on equality and the solidarity of its member peoples' (article 1), and that its institutions are founded on 'the common ideal of liberty, equality and fraternity, and are designed to permit of democratic evolution' (Preamble). Member States have the right to

> self-administration and the free and democratic management of their affairs. There is only one citizenship throughout the Community. All citizens are equal in law, whatever their origin, race or religion. They have the same duties. (Article 77.)

Territories within the Republic

The Community consists of the French Republic and 12 other member-States. The French Republic consists of the Overseas Territories, or former Colonies, Algeria, the Saharan *départements* and the four overseas *départements* of Guadeloupe, Martinique, Réunion and Guyana, sometimes referred to as the 'old Colonies', since they are the oldest of the French possessions.[1] These enjoyed universal suffrage as far back as 1848. Since the beginning of the Third Republic they have enjoyed it without interruption, electing both Deputies and Senators to the French Parliament. In 1946, at their own request, their administration was assimilated to that of France. Since then, they have constituted four *départements*, with Prefects, General Councils, *communes* and Mayors, administered exactly as are French metropolitan *départements*, except where

---

[1] TheConstitution does not, in fact, mention by name either Algeria or the four Overseas *départements*. Nor did that of the Fourth Republic. But *Titre* XI (articles 72–8) is held to apply to all of them. *v. infra* pp. 174–5, and 184–5, however, on the uncertainties regarding the status of Algeria.

special provisions are necessitated by their geographical remoteness or their economic backwardness. Unless provisions are expressly made to the contrary, all French legislation applies to them automatically.

The four overseas *départements* retain this status under the Fifth Republic and continue to elect ten Deputies and seven Senators to the French Parliament. It does not seem that the Constitution allows of any further evolution, though article 73 provides for any adaptations of their 'legislative régime or administrative organization' that may be necessary in view of their particular situation.

The 18 Overseas Territories were offered a choice of four courses of action, of which three were laid down in the Constitution (article 76) and the fourth in a verbal undertaking by General de Gaulle. They could decide, within four months of the promulgation of the Constitution (article 91), either to retain the status of Overseas Territories, as modified by the 1956 'outline-law', or they could be assimilated to France, as are the overseas *départements*, or they could become member-States of the Community, a new status which offered them greater possibilities of self-administration immediately and the possibility of further evolution, not excluding ultimate independence (article 86). Alternatively, in accordance with the verbal undertaking given by General de Gaulle during his tour of the Overseas Territories before the constitutional referendum, they could become independent immediately, by the simple process of voting 'No' in the referendum, which would be interpreted by France as a desire to leave the community. No Overseas Territory chose the first of these possibilities. Only one, Guinea, chose the fourth and consequently became an independent Republic on 2nd October 1958. Seven West African Territories, the four Equatorial African Territories and Madagascar became member-States, and five, namely, St. Pierre-et-Miquelon, the Comoro Archipelago, French Somaliland, Polynesia and New Caledonia, chose to retain the status of Overseas Territories.

These five territories are thus, like the overseas *départements*, administered under the Fifth Republic exactly as they were under the Fourth. The Overseas Territories will be able to take advantage of the possibilities of evolution contained in the 1956 'outline-law', but the Constitution does not appear to envisage any further evolution towards independence. The Territories are, in any case, small and poor. The largest, the Comoro Archipelago, has a population of about 180,000, the smallest, St. Pierre-et-Miquelon, only 4,000. As in the case of the four overseas *départements*, the Overseas Territories are offered the possibility of some modification of their organization (article 74), 'taking into account their special interests within the general interests of the Republic' and such modifications may be carried out by law, that is without involving the necessity for constitutional revision. Since the office of Minister for Overseas Territories no longer exists, they are dealt with by the Minister-Delegate who is also responsible for the Saharan regions and for the utilization of atomic energy.[1]

The Trustee Territories

The two trustee territories of Togoland and the Cameroons, though not French possessions, were administered throughout most of the Fourth Republic as Overseas Territories, and elected representatives to the French Parliament. From 1956 onwards, they moved rapidly towards independence. By 1958, each had a 'Statute' and an elected Parliament and was virtually self-governing. Both acceded to independence in 1960. During the interim period their relations with France were dealt with under the agreements of February 1958, which meant that France retained responsibility for diplomacy, defence and currency and was represented in the Territories by a High Commissioner. Neither Togoland nor the Cameroons voted in the 1958 referendum or elections.

The Member-States of the Community

Along with the Republic, the Community comprises the 12 new member-States. Their choice of this status was made in each case

[1] The French-protected Pacific islands of Wallis and Futuna voted on 27th. December 1959 in favour of transfer to the status of Overseas Territory.

by a decision of the Territorial Assembly, taken during November and December 1958. The Territories then announced the names by which they wished to be known and drew up Constitutions which were submitted for the approval of the Territorial Assemblies. General elections were then held for the first legislative Assemblies of the new States.

Responsibility for the administration of the member-States is divided between the Community and the States. The Community is responsible for foreign policy, defence, currency, economic and financial matters of common concern and of 'the policy relating to strategic raw materials'. The Community also exercises general control over justice, higher education and the general organization of external communications, except where special agreements decide otherwise. Member-States are free to make special agreements with the Community, either creating new fields of common administration, or transferring matters from common administration to that of a single State.

The main organs of the Community are three. The Executive Council consists of the French Prime Minister and the Heads of the Governments of member-States, together with the Ministers entrusted by the President of the Community with responsibility for Community affairs. Its function is to discuss general policy and to ensure co-ordination between the different Governments within the Community. It discusses, for instance, the distribution between member-States of the financial burden of common administration. The Senate consists of delegates from the French Parliament and from the legislative Assemblies of member-States.[1] Its functions

[1] Senators for the Community are chosen for not more than five years, their period of office being coterminous with their period of office as Senators or Deputies. They possess the traditional Parliamentary immunities.

Representation in the Senate of the Community is as follows:

(a) The French Republic: 186 members, half chosen by the Assembly and half by the Senate. These were, in July 1959:

77 Deputies and 76 Senators representing	Metropolitan France
12 ,, ,, 12 ,, ,,	Algeria and the Sahara
2 ,, ,, 2 ,, ,,	the Overseas *départements*
2 ,, ,, 3 ,, ,,	the Overseas Territories.

include discussion of economic and financial matters concerning the Community, before Bills in these fields are voted on by either the French Parliament or the State Assemblies, and examination of international agreements or Treaties affecting the Community. It may take binding decisions on matters concerning which authority has been expressly delegated to it by legislative Assemblies of member-States. Such decisions are promulgated in the same way as laws of the different Territories. The Court of Arbitration[1] decides disputes arising between members of the Community, regarding either the interpretation or the application of Constitutional provisions or organic laws, or agreements affecting the Community, or on such other matters as member-States agree to submit to it. Its decisions are binding. The Court also pronounces, at the request of the President, on the regularity of appointment of delegates to the Senate of the Community.

The President of the Community

By far the most important power in the Community is that of the President of the Republic, acting in his capacity of President of the Community. Presidents of the Fourth Republic were *ex-officio* Presidents of the French Union, as Presidents of the Fifth are also Presidents of the Community. But there are at least two significant differences. Presidents of the Fourth Republic were elected solely by Deputies and Senators of the French Parliament, of whom overseas representatives constituted about one in six. Presidents of the Fifth Republic are elected by a special electoral college which

(*b*) The member-States: 98 members, made up of Madagascar 17, Sudan 13, Upper Volta 12, the Ivory Coast 11, Niger 9, Sénégal 8, Dahomey 6, Mauretania 3, Chad 9, Central Africa 4, Congo and Gaboon 3 each. In addition each member-State is to send two representatives to act when required as spokesmen before the Economic and Social Council.

[1] The Court consists of seven judges, chosen for six years by the President of the Community from among persons with at least ten years' experience as members of either judicial or administrative Tribunals, or as teachers in University Law Faculties, or with twenty years' experience if their juridical qualifications are of a different type.

ncludes, along with members of Parliament and representatives of ocal authorities, representatives of both legislative and local Assemblies of Overseas Territories, and representatives of member-States of the Community. [1]

Second, in his capacity as President of the Community, the President of the Republic has considerable real power, whereas Presidents of the French Union were merely ceremonial figure-heads. The President is represented in each member-State by a High Commissioner, appointed by him.[2] He presides over meetings of the Executive Council, convenes it, decides its agenda and the place where meetings are to be held. He nominates the Secretary-General responsible for directing and co-ordinating the work of the Council, and appoints the staff of his Secretariat, which is responsible to him. He also 'formulates and notifies' the measures to be taken as a result of Council meetings and is responsible for seeing that they are carried out. He sees that the provisions contained in the Constitution, organic laws concerning the Community, decisions of the Court of Arbitration, and Treaties and agreements of the Community are respected. He convenes the Senate, may decide to convene it in extraordinary or (with the assent of a tenth of its members) in secret session, decides whether or not to consult it on questions not specifically laid down as being its concern, in parti-cular, on social, economic and cultural questions. In cases where the

[1] In practice, however, this meant that overseas representatives were *less* strongly represented in the electoral College electing General de Gaulle than they would have been under the former system, owing to the predominance in the electoral College of the representatives of small towns of metropolitan France. In a College of 81,761, 76,310 represented metropolitan France and only 3,439 the member-States, a proportion of about one to 23. Over half of the electoral College consisted of representatives of French villages with under ,500 inhabitants. This disparity could, of course, be corrected for the election of subsequent Presidents, since the representation of member-States is deter-mined by agreement with France (article 6). At the time of the election of General de Gaulle, they were represented in the electoral College on the same basis as the Overseas Territories of the Republic.

[2] Some of President de Gaulle's appointments were clearly made without consulting the State in question.

Senate has taken binding decisions,[1] or where laws have been passed revising the Constitution or organic laws relating to the Community, it is the President who decides whether the matter is urgent enough for promulgation within a week, instead of the normal period of a month. His powers are even more extensive where the Court of Arbitration is concerned. Its seven judges, who sit for six years, are all appointed by him (thought he cannot dismiss them). He may seek the Court's advice on any question concerning the Community which relates to interpretation of the Constitution or of organic laws, and the reply communicated to him by the Court will not be published.

These powers constitute a formidable list. The President is, indeed, at present the sole authority of the Community with the power to take binding decisions. Since these decisions are binding on the French Republic, as well as on other member-States, it is important to know something of the circumstances in which they are taken. Yet neither the Constitution, nor the four organic laws governing the composition and functions of the organs of the Community, give any guidance on this point. Until the Community has established its own precedents, until the lines along which it is likely to evolve are clearer, and until Presidential acts, as distinct from those of the first President, have also accumulated their own precedents, the nature of the office constitutes a series of question-marks. Who really takes the decisions which are 'formulated and notified' by the President? Does he convey 'the sense of the meeting'? Or can he 'complete and define' any decisions (to use the vocabulary of article 34), or 'formulate and notify' his own, if the meeting fails to reach agreement? So far, discussions in the Executive Council are surrounded by the kind of secrecy that characterizes British Cabinet meetings.

The problem of the relationship between Community policy and French policy is also wrapped in obscurity. In theory, the President is free to appoint Ministers for Common Affairs who are not Ministers in the French Government. But since France will be

[1] This is possible only by express delegation on the part of the legislative Assemblies of the Community (article 83).

n practice, responsible for these subjects, it would be ridiculous to magine two Ministers for Finance or Foreign Affairs, one for the Community and one for France. So long as French citizens are to be called on to pay for both Community defence and Community economic development, 'Common Affairs' must mean French affairs, in which case, the appointment by the President is a pure formality. What happens if the French Parliament passes a law conflicting with a decision announced by the President? Since the President's job as arbitrator includes advice to, and possibly action affecting, the French Government, as well as arbitration in the interests of the Community, how does he ensure that his two selves remain distinct? These are only a few of the uncertainties surrounding the whole concept of the Community.

Uncertainties of the Community

What the Community will become cannot, in the nature of things, be apparent for some time. Almost a year elapsed before the institutions, as provided for in the Constitution, organic laws and decrees, were actually in place. The Executive Council met six times between February and December 1959, but was largely occupied in deciding on its methods of work. The Senate could not be constituted until the member-States had drawn up their Constitutions, had them approved and elected their legislative Assemblies. These processes continued throughout the first half of 1959, and the Senate met for the first time on 15th July 1959. It required time, too, for the considerable administrative reorganization necessitated by the creation of the Community to be carried out. For instance, functions formerly carried out by the Minister for Overseas France, or by the federal organs of West and Equatorial Africa, and now belonging to Governments of member-States had to be transferred, and others had to be transferred to the seven Ministries for Community Affairs.[1] These, and the holders of other offices such as, for

[1] These were announced in February 1959. They were the Ministers for Foreign Affairs, Economic and financial policy, Justice, Higher Education, Transport, Telecommunications and Defence all of whom were holders of these portfolios in the French Government.

L

instance, the Secretary-General of the Community, the Minister of State for Technical Assistance to member-States, the Minister-Delegate responsible for the Sahara, had all to work out their precise relations to each other.[1] There was, in the early stages, a great deal of administrative improvisation and there were also some constitutional uncertainties. For instance, the Constitution does not list, among the articles under which the President of the Republic can act without a counter-signature, those dealing with the Community, though President de Gaulle has certainly dispensed with a counter-signature. Indeed, as constitutional lawyers have pointed out, if the President, acting in his capacity as President of the Community, were to exercise his very considerable powers only with the counter-signature of a Minister of the Republic, then attempts to present the Community as a family, or a quasi-federation of States would be jeopardized from the start, and member-States would be tempted to argue that 'the Community' was merely a new name for an old and unsatisfactory relationship.

But the institutional problems are only a first step. The fundamental necessity is the establishment of a working relationship whose spirit will be regarded by the member-States as consistent with their new status. The Community is a unique experiment. As M. Debré has pointed out, it is not a federation, nor is it a Commonwealth. It lacks the basic national unity characteristic of the former

[1] Differences of status of African Territories, as well as the tremendous economic problems, created considerable administrative complications. Relations with Guinea were dealt with by the Minister for Foreign Affairs, those with Togo and the Cameroons by a Minister of State. A new office of Minister-Adviser was announced in May, 1959. Minister-Advisers were intended to act as advisers of the French Government on matters concerning the Community (they could, if necessary, be asked to attend French Cabinet meetings), and possibly also as representatives of the Community on French delegations at international conferences or on international bodies. They were to hold office, in the first place for a year, with the possibility of re-appointment. Four were appointed in July, 1959. They were MM. Senghor (President of the Assembly of Mali), Houphouet-Boigny (Prime Minister of the Ivory Coast), Lisette (Vice-President of the Government of Chad) and Tsiranana (President of the Republic of Madagascar).

and the juridical equality characteristic of the latter. What it *is* will become apparent only as the 13 members learn to work together. As provided for on paper, it is only a framework to be filled in by concrete acts and specific attitudes.

At present, there are, at least, five major political uncertainties. The first concerns France's intentions. Is the Community to be, as article 86 implies, a route leading by peaceful evolution from partial autonomy to eventual independence? This is what most of the member-States intend it to be. M. Senghor, leader of the *Parti du Regroupement Africain*, which at its Cotonou Conference in July 1958 had voted in favour of immediate independence, stated in January 1959:

> We are ready to remain in the Community, if the Community allows us to attain a threefold objective: federations of West and Equatorial African States; independence by stages; and an association with France on a confederal basis. A dynamic interpretation of the Constitution would make all this possible.

Will France's interpretation be 'dynamic' in this sense? On paper, enormous powers are entrusted to the President of the Community, while the executive and deliberative organs remain in essence advisory bodies. It is the President of the Republic who formulates and communates the decisions of meetings of the Executive Council. And the Senate's decisions are binding only in matters on which powers have been expressly delegated to it by member-States; which means that powers at present exercised by France can be transferred to the organs of the Community only with her consent. In any case the Senate meets for only two sessions a year, each of them lasting no more than a month.

The evolution of the Community will proceed, therefore, at a pace either set, or agreed to, willingly or unwillingly, by France. A restrictive interpretation of the Constitutional provisions could mean in practice, a status for the new States very like the one created by the *loi-cadre* of 1956, which they feel they have outgrown. The Senate, for instance, could remain a purely advisory organ whose importance would be even less than was that of the Assembly of the Union under the Fourth Republic. That body included a number of Councillors with real expertise in colonial matters, and its debates were often of a high quality, but its influence on the policy of French Governments was negligible. The representation of the different member-States in the Senate is determined on the basis of population and the degree of responsibility within the Community,[1] which means in practice that, of its 284 members, almost two-thirds (186) are chosen by the French National Assembly and Senate. A detailed study of the organization of the work of the Executive Council reveals a complicated machinery of specialized Committees dealing with the different aspects of Community affairs (economic and financial matters, transport, relations of the Community with other international organizations, justice, higher education), but these appear to be no more than study groups submitting reports to the Executive Council. It would be possible for it to be little more than a periodic meeting of heads of Governments and Ministers for Community Affairs, at which decisions taken in reality by France are commented on, and either formally approved by the heads of Government of member-States or 'formulated and notified' to them by the President of the Community, with or without their consent.

If the chief danger, on the French side, is a restrictive interpretation, based on too rigid and juridical an approach, or on the survival of colonialist bureaucratic attitudes, the chief danger from the African side is a desire to move too fast, and in several contradictory directions at once. Demands for premature independence may be stimulated by the achievement of independence by Nigeria, Togoland and the Cameroons. There are already indications that some States are thinking in terms of independence within a few years. As early as July 1959, some delegates at the constitutive Congress of the P.F.A. (*Parti de la Fédération Africaine*) wanted to press for independence in 1960. In September 1959, Mali decided to

[1] In practice, representation in the 1959 Senate was decided purely on a population basis.

become independent in the immediate future,[1] but to remain closely linked with France within an association of a semi-federal nature.

Among the growing pains of African nationalism, three political tendencies are already creating difficulties. First, most of the territories are poor, in both human and material resources, and their frontiers are often artificial, cutting across racial boundaries. They are aware of the need for union but disagreed on the best methods of achieving it. The *Parti du Regroupement Africain* (P.R.A.), itself formed by the fusion of a number of parties, fears what its leaders call 'the Balkanization of Africa', and so favours the creation of 'primary federations' of African States, which would become the basic units of association with France. A first move in that direction was made in April 1959, with the setting up of the institutions of Mali, a federation formed by Senegal and Sudan. The *Rassemblement Démocratique Africain* (R.D.A.) led by M. Houphouet-Boigny, Prime Minister of the Ivory Coast, is conscious mainly of the need to foster the links with France, on whose massive economic aid the viability of the new African States depends.

> A union of poverties, (said M. Houphouet-Boigny), will not produce abundance. . . . Why consider regroupings that are without either economic power or cultural influence?

His solution is, therefore, the creation of a Franco-African Community, based on direct links between each State and France, though he approves of economic co-operation between African States through a Customs Union.[2]

---

[1] Mali is contemplating using the procedure provided for under article 78 rather than that provided for under article 86. The former lays down that matters dealt with by the Community can be transferred to the competence of individual States by agreement. Mali proposes simply that responsibility for *all* affairs shall be so transferred.

[2] The Federation of Mali was primarily political in inspiration. The economic interests of the two territories are divergent, Sudan being much more backward than Sénégal. The *Conseil d'Entente*, aiming at a Customs Union between the Ivory Coast, Upper Volta, Dahomey and Niger, and announced

This approach is also partly determined by fear of the third tendency, namely the growth of pan-Africanism. Some African States are already looking beyond a Franco-African Community. The independent Republic of Guinea, while remaining in the franc zone and not having yet ruled out the possibility of a form of association with France,[1] announced in November 1958 the intention to form a Union with Ghana. Mali, too, seemed to be contemplating this possibility.

> Our aim, (said M. Senghor), is the constitution of a negro-African nation, an entity cutting across artificial frontiers and tribal diversity.[2]

A third uncertainty arises from the fact that the States depend for survival on the continuance (and, indeed, increase) both of the already large subsidies that France has provided since the war for their economic and social development, and also of the supply of French technicians, administrators and teachers, until the States can train a minimum of African *cadres*. It is doubtful whether France can provide either on the scale needed and, at the same time, carry out her ambitious plan for economic, social and administrative levelling-up in Algeria. Some opponents of the Constitution argued that General de Gaulle's offer of immediate independence to those

in April 1959 as a countermove to the setting up of Mali, was primarily economic in inspiration, though co-operation was, in fact, closer than that between the two States of Mali. In June 1959 the four members decided, at Sahel-Bénin, to co-ordinate their financial, judicial and administrative systems, and also health and labour legislation and communications.

The four Equatorial African States have also formed a Customs Union.

[1] 'Association' between France and other countries is provided for by article 88 of the Constitution, but the article contains nothing beyond this bare statement.

[2] The P.F.A. (*Parti de la Fédération Africaine*) was set up at Dakar in July 1959 with the aim of transforming the Community, as soon as possible, into a 'multi-national Confederation'. The members of the Sahel-Bénin Union rejected this idea, which, in the words of M. Houphouet-Boigny, would 'make the Community no more than a Commonwealth'.

States that chose to vote *No* in the constitutional referendum was unreal and, in effect, a form of political blackmail, because the States were well aware that their economic dependence on France ruled out this course of action.[1] But that economic dependence could be a two-edged weapon. Demands by States for economic aid as a condition of their continued membership of the Community could not only encourage friction with each other, but place an intolerable burden on France.

A fourth uncertainty is that created by the political immaturity of the States themselves and their consequent political instability. The two main parties are both, in their present form, recent creations. Rivalry between them is intense and has been, at times, very violent. There is rivalry between trade union organizations, which had already led to schism in 1959 in the most important of them, the *Union Génerale du Travailleurs de l'Afrique Noire* (U.G.T.A.N.), in which M. Sekou Touré's influence was strong and had created suspicion in neighbouring territories. There are also personal rivalries between political leaders, and tribal rivalries.

As yet, in spite of the existence in each State of legislative Assemblies and Governments headed by Prime Ministers, the infrastructure of Parliamentary government is lacking. The electoral results in these territories themselves provide eloquent evidence of immaturity. Majorities in the referendum ranged from 78 per cent to over 99 per cent. Of the 12 former Overseas Territories, now member-States, ten produced majorities of over 90 per cent, and one a majority of 99·9 per cent. The percentage of the electorate voting ranged from just over 37 per cent to 98 per cent. In each case, opinion echoed that of the national leaders, virtually all of whom have represented their Territories in Paris—in the National Assembly, the Senate, the Assembly of the Union, or the Economic Council. The one Territory that seceded also followed its leader, M. Sekou Touré, and there, 95 per cent of the voters voted *No*.

[1] *v.* for instance, the admission by M. Tsiranana of Madagascar in August 1958: 'My feelings lead me to favour total and immediate independence. My reason tells me that that is impossible.'

The fifth uncertainty is only indirectly related to France's relations with the member-States, but could be important in influencing the atmosphere in which problems arising between France and the new States are dealt with. African nationalism is sympathetic to Algerian nationalism, and the failure of the Fifth Republic to solve the Algerian problem could, therefore, seriously impair relations within the Franco-African Community.

Prospects of the Community

At the moment an important experiment has begun, and what is more, it has begun in an atmosphere of goodwill. It will need both patience and goodwill to overcome the inevitable tensions that must arise between members of an association, who differ in race, religion and language and whose formal equality with each other is recognized by all to be very largely a fiction, in view of their common dependence on the dominant partner, the French Republic. The Republic is dominant, not merely in wealth and political experience, but also numerically in the different organs of the Community, politically in important fields of policy, including defence and foreign affairs, and constitutionally, in that changes of status are not matters between the State and the Community as a whole, but between each State and one other member, the French Republic. Since the Republic is also the former colonial power, the difficulties in the way of psychological 'decolonialization' are tremendous.

The first task must be to create an atmosphere of equality, as far as possible, given the unavoidable realities of the situation. Some steps have already been taken, quite clearly with this in mind. The provision for representation of member-States on diplomatic delegations, the holding of the fourth Executive Council meeting in Madagascar, instead of in Paris, and of the sixth in St Louis-du-Sénégal in the Republic of Mali, the association of the member-States with the celebration of 14th July—all these do not make the fiction of equality any less fictional, but to African opinion, still sensitive to, and obsessed by, the danger of colonialism, such indications of status can make the reality more bearable.

In this context, the President of the Community can probably do a great deal. General de Gaulle has himself experienced the frustration of representing a nation without status, resources or authority. France was, during the war, in a state of temporary eclipse only, while the African States have barely emerged as States, but the feelings expressed by General de Gaulle in a conversation with Sir Winston (then Mr) Churchill during the war could well represent those of the Prime Minister of a member-State, vis-a-vis the Government of France:

> You have behind you (said General de Gaulle), a strong State, a compact nation, a united Europe, large armies. What are my resources? Yet, as you know, I am responsible for the interests and the future of France. The burden is too heavy, and I am too poor to be subservient.[1]

It would be interesting to know how far, in meetings of the Executive Council, for instance, the attitude of General de Gaulle as President of the Community—*le style du Général*, as it is fashionable to call it—has helped to efface some of the unhappier African memories of contacts with French colonial officialdom.

The constitutional provisions help in three ways to create the conditions for a better atmosphere. Whatever the economic pressures, in *form*, and that is in itself an important element of status, membership of the Community was an offer that Africans were free to accept or refuse; it was not imposed by France, as previous reforms have been. Nor did Africans regard the difficulties between France and Guinea, immediately following the referendum, in the same light as some British observers did, that is, as evidence of France's intention to honour the General's undertaking as grudgingly as possible. There was, on the contrary, a strong feeling among some of the new member-States that Guinea should not appear to have profited from secession by securing immediately and, as of right, economic or technical aid that member-States had paid for, in

[1] *Mémoires de Guerre*, I (Plon, 1954), p. 209.

some cases by postponing for an indefinite time their hopes of independence.

The second, and most vital constitutional provision is the right to independence at any time. This has since been categorically re-affirmed by General de Gaulle, in particular, in a speech made in Madagascar:

> The Community (he said), is a group of free States, which have decided to co-operate in liberty and in solidarity. They retain their freedom to go their own way at any time, but they have decided not to exercise that freedom, but to remain together in order to carry through a great human venture.[1]

The third important characteristic of the constitutional provisions is their flexibility. The degree of autonomy of each State, the nature of its relationship with France, the functions of the Executive Council, the powers of the Senate of the Community—all these can be adapted in the light of the situation in different States and in the light of the evolution of African opinion. Precision and rigidity, which so often characterize French constitutional relationships, have been abandoned for pragmatism. Even changes in the constitutional provisions governing the Community as a whole (articles 77 to 87, constituting *Titre* XII) can be made by means of an ordinary law, voted in the same terms by the Parliament of the Republic and the Senate of the Community.[2]

[1] Speech of 7th July, 1959. Article 86 provides for 'changes of status' and adds that a State 'may become independent in the same conditions'. These conditions are (a) a request for a change of status demanded either by the Republic, or by a State and, in the latter case, the request must take the form of a resolution voted in the legislative Assembly and confirmed by a referendum; and (b) an agreement on the methods by which the change of status is to be applied, which must be approved by both the Parliament of the Republic and the legislative Assembly of the State concerned. This provision could be used so as to give France an effective right of veto.

[2] There was an ambiguity in article 85 (which governs the revision of the organization of the Community as a whole) and articles 82, 83, and 84 providing for the setting up of the organs of the Community by organic laws.

A French expert on French overseas problems wrote in 1951:

> The English manage to leave at the right time, and are discovered later to be still there—unofficially—and as influential as they ever were. The French have confidence only in written documents and continue to cling to them even when the world has changed.[1]

That criticism need not any longer be true, but the responsibility for seizing the new opportunities is one that is shared by both French and African partners in the new experiment.

Article 85 exempts *Titre* XII from the application of article 89, but not explicitly from the application of article 46 governing the amendment of organic laws. Article 21 of the organic law (Nº 58–1255) of 19th December, 1958, settles this point by providing that organic laws dealing with the Community shall be revised under the procedure laid down in article 85.

[1] Charles-André Julien, *L'Afrique du Nord en marche* (Paris, Julliard, 1953), p. 403.

CHAPTER X

Algeria

The 1958 Constitution, as has already been said, makes no mention of Algeria. Nor indeed did that of 1946. Both refer only to 'Overseas *départements*' without specifying any by name. The result has been some uncertainty regarding the precise constitutional status of Algeria. While the nationalist rebellion continues, the question is in a sense purely academic. From 1955 onwards, Algeria has been administered under a series of emergency regulations. In 1958, the revolution of 13th May resulted in the assumption by the Commander-in-Chief in Algeria of full civil and military powers and it was not until the end of the year that steps were taken effectively to restore some degree of civilian authority.

In spite of these facts, a brief account of Algerian administration, and of the changes carried out during the Fourth Republic and since, may help to explain the different attitudes of Frenchmen towards the Algerian problem and, in particular, the reasons for their attachment to, or rejection of, certain possible solutions of it.

The background

Algeria constitutes a unique experiment in assimilation. It has been French for over 130 years and never, before that time or since, has it been in any real sense a nation. The former North African Protectorates were nations with a long history and with their own rulers and systems of government, when they came under French rule. Moroccans and Tunisians were never regarded by the French as Frenchmen. Algerians have been, and still are, French, in the sense that this is the only national status that they have ever had. They can enter and leave France without formalities. Some 300,000 to 400,000 Moslem Algerians normally work in France, where they are paid at French rates. They have continued to do so (though the numbers have fallen somewhat) throughout the period of rebellion. If they fulfil the residence and registration requirements, they can vote in French elections.

Nationalist movements existed in Algeria from the thirties onward, but they have never had either the unity or the influence of the Tunisian Néo-Destour, or the Moroccan Istiqlal. Rival nationalist movements have carried on permanent bitter and violent feuds, and assassination of members of one by those of another is common. Up to as late as 1955, moreover, a considerable number of the Moslem élite were seeking, not independence from France, but more complete assimilation. They wanted to be, not Algerians, but first-class, rather than second-class Frenchmen, *des Français à part entière*. How far there is still any real desire on the part of educated Moslems for assimilation, or for 'integration' (a new term emphasizing the need for real equality of the two communities, European and Moslem, within the French Republic) it is difficult to say whilst nationalist terrorism on the one hand, and the presence of the French army on the other, prevent the free expression of opinion. The fact that many thousands of Moslems have agreed to serve on local Councils at the risk of their lives, and that they have continued to do so in spite of the murder of a number by the rebels, indicates, at least, that a considerable section of the Moslem community is willing to co-operate with France.

Throughout the Third Republic, the administration of Algeria was based on the principle of assimilation. The fertile coastal strip, some hundred miles wide, which contains the majority of the population, was divided into three *départements*, Algiers, Oran and Constantine. Each had its Council, its Prefect, its *communes* and *Maires*, supervised, as French local Government authorities are, by the Ministry of the Interior. Algerian Deputies and Senators (representing only the European and assimilated population) sat in the French Parliament, where they joined French parties.

Is Algeria French?

It was not until 1946, with the creation of the four Overseas *départe-ments*—a new status, involving complete assimilation—that the problem of the precise constitutional status of Algeria really arose. Up to then, it had been taken for granted that Algeria was French, as she had been since the French occupation in the 1830's. Under the Fourth Republic, it was maintained by some Frenchmen, how-ever, that the Algerian *départements* should be classed as Overseas *départements*,[1] and by others that they were French *départements*. During the debates preceding the vote of the Algerian statute, there was a great deal of legal hair-splitting on this issue. It was pointed out, for instance, in support of the second thesis, that the 1946 Constitution provided for the automatic application of French legislation to the Overseas *départements*, unless specific exceptions were made, whereas not all French laws were automatically appli-cable in Algeria.[2] In fact, both Algeria and the four Overseas *départements* were French in the sense that they were part of the French Republic, and that, throughout the Fourth Republic, their populations were French citizens who enjoyed universal suffrage and elected representatives to the French Parliament. There were, nevertheless, certain differences between Algerian administration and that of the Overseas *départements* and also between the admini-stration of Algerian *départements* and of those of metropolitan France.[3] Algeria constituted an entity, in that a Governor-General

[1] This was the view of the *Conseil d'Etat* in an *avis* of the 27th March 1947.

[2] The argument that Algerian *départements* were French was put, in parti-cular, by an Algerian professor of law M. E. Viard, *v. Caractères politiques et le régime législatif de l'Algérie. Bibliothèque de la Faculté de droit d'Alger, volume III* (Recueil Sirey, 1948).

[3] The three *départements* of Alsace-Lorraine also present certain special features, in particular the existence of Catholic State schools (since these *départements* are still governed in religious matters by the *Concordat*).

(from 1956–8, a Minister-residing in Algeria) represented the Government of the Republic throughout the territory, and in that Algerian administration (except for the Departments of War, Justice and Education, which were run directly from Paris) was centralized in Algiers under the authority of the Governor-General. Algeria also had, up to 1958, a special electoral régime. The two communities, European and Moslem, voted in separate colleges, some eight to nine million Moslems electing the same number of Deputies as the million or so Europeans and assimilated Moslems. This discrimination existed also in local Government.[1]

Administrative changes during the Fourth Republic

Algeria was certainly, therefore, to some extent a special case. Whether it should be regarded as a group of French or as a group of Overseas *départements* would have been a question of no significance, except to lawyers, if it had not been that, with the prolongation of the nationalist rebellion, the European population in Algeria became more and more determined that Algeria must remain for ever 'indissolubly linked' to France. Those who held, and who continue to hold, this view, attach importance to juridical arguments as constituting evidence of the legitimacy of their claim. Algeria's status is, in principle, that laid down in the Algerian Statute of 1947, namely:

[1] The distinction between Moslems and Europeans is not racial but legal. Europeans are those whose affairs are dealt with under the French Civil Code. Moslems are subject to Koranic law. Assimilated Moslems are those who have renounced their status and accepted the obligations of French civil law (which means, in effect, renouncing their religion). Before the war, only those who came under the French Civil Code were citizens. The 1946 Constitution made all Algerians citizens and, therefore, electors. Discrimination was based on the civil status, *citoyens de statut civil local* (Moslems) voting in separate colleges from *citoyens de statut civil de droit commun* (Europeans and assimilated Moslems). All electoral distinctions were abolished in 1958, though the term 'Moslem' is still used unofficially, applying to all those whose affairs are dealt with under Koranic law. The electoral law, though it includes provisions for fixed numbers of Moslem candidates, nowhere uses the word 'Moslem'.

> . . . a group of *départements*, enjoying corporate personality
> financial autonomy and a special organization. . . . All inhabitants
> of French nationality in the *départements* of Algeria enjoy, with-
> out distinction of origin, race, language or religion, the rights
> attached to French citizenship, and are subject to the same
> obligations.[1]

The movement in favour of 'integration' which developed at the
end of the Fourth Republic appeared to be in favour of an even
more complete assimilation of Algerian to French administration, as
soon as peace was restored.

Throughout the Fourth Republic, however, Algeria continued
to be treated both as French, and as French with a difference. The
Statute of 1947 set up an elected Assembly, consisting of 60 Moslem
and 60 European members, whose President was to be Moslem one
year and European the next. Its function was to supervise financial
administration, to give advice to the Government regarding the
application or adaptation of French legislation to Algeria, and
regarding special executive measures that might be called for in
Algeria. It had no powers of decision, and it remained largely ineffective, partly because Moslems elected to it were often more
representative of French than they were of Moslem opinion, and
partly because French Governments did not apply those sections of
the Statute which provided for increasing Moslem responsibility in
the administration. It was always possible for the European representatives to avoid being outvoted, since on the demand of 25 per
cent of the members of the Assembly, or of the Finance Commission
or of the Governor-General, a special two-thirds majority could be
required. Elections were, by general admission, manipulated by the
administration. And the arrest of a number of nationalists before
the first renewal of the Assembly in 1951 resulted in their loss of
over half the small number of seats they already had. By 1952 a
considerable section of opinion, belonging to different nationalist
organizations, had decided that co-operation with France within

[1] *Statut de l'Algérie* 1947, articles 1 and 2.

this framework was no longer possible. By 1954, nationalism had taken the form of armed insurrection.

The Algerian Assembly was finally dissolved in 1956, but, by then most of the Moslem members had already resigned, some, no doubt, owing to intimidation by the rebels, but others because they now wanted independence. The outbreak of the rebellion really marks the end of the purely assimilative experiment. From then onwards, until the revolution of 13th May, French Governments tried, at one and the same time, to end the rebellion by military action, to increase the real possibilities of Moslem participation in government, and to make some concessions to what was called the 'Algerian personality',[1] without severing any of the fundamental links binding Algeria to France.

From 1956 onwards, in spite of the rebellion (and also partly because of it) France began to carry out a series of administrative reforms. First, local government was reorganized. Only a minority of Municipal Councils had been fully elective on the French pattern and even these (in the *communes de plein exercice*) had reserved three-fifths of the seats for Europeans. In the less evolved *communes* (*communes mixtes*) local Councils had included nominated Moslem representatives and had had considerably fewer powers. The process of transforming all *communes* into *communes de plein exercice* was speeded up, and over 1,000 new ones were created. Pending the holding of elections, seats were provisionally filled by nominated 'special delegations'. The number of *départments* was increased, first to four (Bône was created in 1955) then to 12, and, in April 1958, to 15.[2] Councils for *départements* were also replaced by specially nominated bodies, in the hope of giving the Moslems confidence that a new start was really being made.

Steps were also taken to increase the number of Moslems employed in the public service and to train more for it. Various economic and social measures were applied, with a view to raising the Moslem standard of living.

---

[1] Recognition of *la personnalité algérienne* does not imply recognition of *la vocation nationale*.   [2] By 1959, only 12 were effectively in existence.

From 1956 to 1958, the French representative in Algeria was a Minister of the French Government, the Minister-residing in Algeria. He carried out the functions of Governor-General, and the powers of the dissolved Algerian Assembly were transferred to him. In fact, during this period, the French Government had full powers to carry out reforms, whatever the Moslems might think of them, while effective control passed progressively into the hands of the military authorities, under a series of emergency measures. The French Government's aim was first to stop the fighting, either by a military victory or by negotiations, then to hold elections and, when there were valid spokesmen for Algeria, to discuss with them the future status of the country. Failure to achieve even the first stage led to further administrative changes, in the form of a new status for Algeria, not negotiated, but laid down by a law voted in 1958 by the French Parliament.

The reform consisted of an electoral law, doing away with the double college, and an outline-law which laid down a new framework for the central administration, replacing the Algerian Statute. No more than a bare summary of its provisions is called for, because the prolongation of the rebellion makes it improbable that the text as voted will ever be applied. It was opposed both by the right-wing parties in France and by settler opinion in Algeria, and the final version was voted only after a considerable watering-down of the original provisions. On the other hand, it was certainly unacceptable even to moderate Moslem opinion. As M. Edgar Faure remarked, after the Government's struggle to overcome right-wing opposition: 'the important thing is not to win over the *Indépendants*, but to win over the Moslems'. In fact, however, Moslem opinion was not consulted, and, indeed, could not easily be consulted while the rebellion continued. Nor were there, at this stage, even any Moslem Deputies in the French Assembly. The dissolution of 1955 had ended the mandate of the 30 Algerian Deputies, but since it was impossible to hold elections in Algeria, their seats had not been filled.

The outline-law provided for regional decentralization. In other words, Algeria remained a collection of *départements*, but these were to be grouped in regions, each with its own administration, consisting, on the one hand, of a democratically elected Assembly with a responsible Government and, on the other, of a Community Council made up of nominated members representing European and Moslem interests in equal numbers. Provision was made for the setting up of federal institutions when half the regional Assemblies had so decided.

There is no doubt that one of the purposes of this proposed division into regions was to weaken national sentiment in Algeria—to check the development of what has been called 'the Algerian personality'. The law also stated that 'Algeria is an integral part of the French Republic'. On the other hand, it comes nearer than any previous legislation had done to providing for something like the kind of limited autonomy possessed by the Overseas Territories under the outline-law of 1956. In 1958, this type of organization would certainly have no longer satisfied even moderate nationalist opinion.

The Saharan regions

The Southern desert regions of Algeria, covering an area ten times the size of the coastal *départements*, were, until the discovery of oil and natural gas, sparsely populated, with a high proportion of nomadic tribes, and had remained predominantly under military rule, though the Algerian Statute provided for their eventual integration in the more evolved regions.

The discovery of vast mineral resources in the Sahara necessitated special administrative arrangements, however, and in 1957, the Saharan region of Algeria was divided into two *départements*, Oasis and Saoura. The Bourgès-Maunoury Government of that year included, for the first time, a Minister for the Sahara, responsible for the organization set up at the beginning of 1957 to provide for the social and economic development of the region (*l'Organisation en Commun des Régions Sahariennes*, or O.C.R.S.). This organization was purely economic and, indeed, was at first not limited to Algeria, but was intended to include the Saharan regions of the Overseas Territories of Mauretania, Sudan, Chad and Niger. *De facto*, if not *de jure*, the Saharan regions became from this date onwards effectively separated from Algeria. The Minister for the Sahara replaced the Minister of the Interior as the effective administrative head of the two *départements*. The outline-law of 1958 did not apply to the Saharan regions.

Developments following General de Gaulle's return to power

The law of 3rd June 1958, which gave full powers for a period of six months to the Government constituted by General de Gaulle, expressly excluded powers in certain fields belonging by constitutional and Republican tradition to Parliament. This exception was rendered ineffective, as far as Algeria was concerned, because a law voted the same day renewed the emergency powers act of 1956 which gave the Government full powers in Algeria. One of the last acts of M. Pflimlin's short-lived Government had been to entrust full military and civilian powers to the Commanding Officer in Algeria, General Salan.[1] After the revolution of 13th May, military authorities replaced the normal civilian heads of the administration in the groups of *départements* (*Igamies*)[2] and *départements*, though they were assisted by civilians. They remained in effective control until December, when a civilian was appointed to the new post of Delegate-General for Algeria (replacing that of Governor-General). He was responsible to the Prime Minister, who took over the functions of the Minister-residing in Algeria. From then on, civilian administration was gradually restored. The Delegate-General exercised full military and civil powers on behalf of the Republic, but the military power was, in fact, delegated to a General as his second-in-command.

Two important developments occurred in 1958, during this

[1] The Minister-residing in Algeria in M. Pflimlin's Government was not able to take up his post owing to the insurrection of 13th May.

[2] Known colloquially as *Igamies* because they are headed by an *Igame*, or *Inspecteur-Général de l'Administration en Mission Extraordinaire*.

period of provisional government. The first was the holding of the constitutional referendum and general, as well as Presidential, elections in Algeria.

The circumstances unfortunately prevented these elections from producing the 'valid spokesman', without which successive Governments had declared negotiations to be impossible. In spite of General de Gaulle's explicit instructions to the Commander-in-Chief, to see that all shades of opinion—the General repeated this phrase, '*je répète, toutes les tendances*'—were free to express themselves, the rebel F.L.N., the *Front de la libération nationale* (which from September 1958 had a provisional Government, with headquarters, for the most part, in Tunis) boycotted the election and threatened those voting with reprisals. No response was made to General de Gaulle's offer to the F.L.N., made shortly before the elections, of negotiations for a cease fire, with a view to achieving peace with honour (*la paix des braves*).

On the other hand, there was undoubted pressure, the extent varying from region to region, by French Army authorities, whose task it was to provide protection for voters (the election dates were staggered to make this possible), to organize the polling booths and often to explain to illiterate Moslems, including women who were voting for the first time, how to cast their votes. In spite of the presence of Civilian Control Commissions to supervise the regularity of the voting, and of regulations governing electoral publicity analagous to those existing in France, the atmosphere alone would have prevented real freedom of expression, even if all accusations of political bias or pressure by the military authorities had been unfounded. The Europeans carried out a campaign in favour of '*l'Algérie française*' and integration, which, in practice, made it impossible for less right-wing candidates to present themselves, and several gave up the attempt on the ground that the conditions were not such as to produce genuine representation of Algerian opinion. Except for those prepared to support the settler position, virtually no Moslem candidates came forward. Of the 50 or so lists of candidates, five were Socialist and, of the rest, all but four were 'integrationist', representing, in the words of one commentator, 'a gamut ranging from Conservative to Fascist'. Of the 21 European and 46 Moslem Deputies elected to represent Algeria, virtually all represented the policy of 'integration'.[1]

The second development was the announcement in October 1958 at Constantine by General de Gaulle himself of a vast five-year plan of economic and social development, in order to fulfil his promise, made on a visit to Algeria immediately after he assumed power, that Moslems would henceforth be *des Français à part entière*. It included the provision of land for farmers, the creation of employment for an additional 400,000 people, housing, education for two children out of every three, and the reservation to Moslems of one tenth of the places in the public service in France and Algeria. It was estimated that a minimum annual expenditure of 100,000 million francs would be required to carry out this programme.

Algeria under the Fifth Republic

The main administrative change under the Fifth Republic concerns the Saharan regions. With the transformation of the Overseas Territories into member-States of the Community, these States ceased to be part of the Republic. The O.C.R.S., therefore, included only the two Saharan *départements*, though any State was free to join the organization by agreement.[2] Saharan affairs were entrusted in the first Government of the Fifth Republic to the Minister-Delegate attached to the Prime Minister, who was also responsible for the affairs of the remaining five Overseas Territories, for the O.C.R.S., and for the organization dealing with atomic energy.[3]

[1] From 1957, French Governments also included one or more Secretaries of State for Algeria, including at least one Moslem. In the first Government of the Fifth Republic, a Moslem woman held office for the first time.

[2] Niger was the first to do so in 1959. On the O.C.R.S., *v. supra*, p. 179.

[3] The *de facto* separation of Algeria and the Sahara was further emphasized by the reference in all official statements to *l'Algérie et le Sahara*, or to *les départements algériens et du Sahara*, and by differences in the electoral system in the two Saharan *départements* (*v. supra*, pp. 62 and 69).

In 1959, local elections were held in Algeria, for the first time since the rebellion, as well as elections to the first Senate of the Fifth Republic. Municipal elections were held in 85 per cent of the 1,485 *Communes*, that is in all of any size; 62 per cent of the electorate voted and nearly 14,000 Councillors were returned, of whom over 11,000 were Moslems. The Senatorial elections resulted in the election of fewer candidates representing the extreme settler views. In general, the tendency was rather to elect former Senators, and, in particular those interested in economic and social questions.

None of the administrative changes carried out during the first year of the Fifth Republic altered the *de facto* relationship of Algeria to France, any more than previous changes had done. They took for granted the continuance of the old assimilative framework. Algeria remained part of the French Republic and was represented as such in the Senate of the Community. Senators and Deputies were elected to the French Parliament. The administration was controlled from Paris. The Delegate-General was the representative of the French Government, responsible directly to the Prime Minister's office. In two minor respects, the links were even strengthened. Bills were passed during the first Parliamentary session of 1959 providing for a common currency in Algeria and France, and the Algerian budget was, at least for the time being, included in that of France. The first had no more than symbolic significance and the second was imposed by the circumstances, for, in the absence of an Algerian Assembly, the French Parliament remained the only place in which Algerians could discuss the budgetary provisions.

For the rest, Algeria remained French with a difference—with a different electoral system and with a standard of living that could not be brought near to that of France within a quarter of a century, even with the aid of a gigantic and crippling financial contribution from France and the provision of teachers, doctors, administrators and technicians, all of whom were urgently needed in France. Integration, the concept of one France from Dunkirk to Tamanrasset, remained, economically as well as politically, as far off as it had been before the revolution of 13th May.[1] In France, the controversy regarding the political future of Algeria remained unresolved, and the war continued in spite of repeated rumours of the growing weakness of the rebel organization and the possibilities of a negotiated ceasefire.

In June 1959, two Algerian Deputies (Europeans representing the settler point of view) put a number of questions to the Prime Minister regarding the *de jure* status of Algeria. In his replies, the Prime Minister reaffirmed that Algeria formed part of the Republic and that, while changes in administrative organization and 'the legislative régime' were provided for under article 73, including the creation, by law, of new territorial divisions for administrative purposes (*collectivités territoriales*), any changes which affected French sovereignty could be made only by way of constitutional revision. The provisions of articles 72 and 73 did not, he said, affect the Algerian Statute, since they related to future, not to past legislation. It would not be constitutionally possible to hold fresh elections in Algeria before 1963, except in the event of a dissolution of the National Assembly, because the organic law governing the composition of the Assembly and the term of office of Deputies provided for the renewal of the total membership of the Assembly at the same time.[2] Similarly, Algerian Senatorial elections could not constitutionally be held before the next date for the partial renewal of the Senate, that is in 1962. The term 'Overseas *départements*', used in

[1] It would be fair to say that the Constantine plan could be interpreted, either as the first stage on the road to economic and social integration, or as an implementation of the policy of aid to under-developed territories, which General de Gaulle frequently mentioned in his speeches.

[2] The Constitution of 1946 also provided for the renewal of the total membership of the Assembly at the same time, but this did not prevent the Government from deciding not to hold elections in Algeria in January 1956. The seats of the 30 Algerian Deputies remained vacant from then until the end of the régime. The constitutionality of this procedure was questioned in some quarters; in others it was defended on the ground that the existence of '*force majeure*' rendering elections in practice impossible constituted a valid defence of the Government's position.

article 73, referred to all *départements* 'situated geographically overseas' and, therefore, included along with the four *départements* of Martinique, Guadeloupe, Guyana and Réunion, those of Algeria and the Sahara.[1]

These statements must be understood as defining effectively, for the time being, the *de jure* status of Algeria and the methods by which it could constitutionally be changed. Not that the Government's views are, as such, authoritative, but the Constitutional Council (whose views on constitutional matters are alone authoritative) can be consulted only on specific legislative or Treaty proposals. Unless or until it is so consulted, the Government of the day remains in practice free to decide, subject to the approval of Parliament, what is or is not constitutional. Any future Government would be equally free to give a different definition.

In reality, neither the *de facto* nor the *de jure* situation of Algeria was relevant to the problem of the future of Algeria, which was a political and a military problem. It had been, more than any other single factor responsible for the end of the Fourth Republic. It was still by no means certain, a year and a half later, that it would not also destroy the Fifth, though General de Gaulle's offer of *autodétermination* on 16th September 1959 provided the first positive step that seemed to offer any reasonable hope of success in bringing the fighting to an end. In essence, this offer was a modification of M. Mollet's 'triptych'—cease-fire, elections, negotiations. This programme had been defeated by the inability of Governments of the Fourth Republic to achieve the first objective. General de Gaulle's Government had reversed the order and begun with elections, only to find a cease-fire equally unattainable.

The offer of *autodétermination* broke new ground in three important ways. First, it handed over responsibility for the choice of Algeria's future political status, in the first place, to the Algerian people. A referendum was to be held in which Algerians would vote for or against independence, or, as General de Gaulle preferred to call it, secession. If secession was rejected, a further referendum

[1] *v. Journal Officiel*, 14th August 1959.

would be held to decide whether Franco-Algerian association was to take the form of assimilation, that is, of integration, or *francisation* as General de Gaulle called it, or, alternatively, of limited self-government, on the basis of internal federalism, the details of which would be worked out by negotiation. General de Gaulle made it clear that this latter form of association was intended by France to be in most ways similar to that between France and the member-States of the Community.

The second change in the situation produced by the offer of *autodétermination* was that it placed responsibility on the rebel organization for bringing the fighting to an end. For, with the possibility of *voting* for independence, the need to go on *fighting* for it disappeared. Voting was to take place within a maximum period of four years from the end of the fighting, peace being regarded as having been achieved when there had been a year in which fewer than 200 people were killed in terrorist attacks. General de Gaulle followed up the declaration with a firm directive to the army in Algeria, in which he emphasized the Government's determination to see that, this time, the consultation would be free from pressure of any kind.

The third change was the insistence on the responsibility of the French people, which would be asked to confirm the choice of the Algerian people. Indeed, General de Gaulle's statement could only be taken to mean that he was, in effect, making such a confirmation a condition of his remaining at the head of affairs.

If the general principles of this offer were unambiguous and courageous, a great deal of essential detail remained to be filled in and there was, therefore, bound to be a period of uncertainty, during which extremist sections on both sides would try to apply pressure, while those hoping for, or trying to avoid negotiations would seek to manœuvre for position. First reactions showed that the 'integrationists' would be powerless to oppose the General on this, unless they could be certain of the backing of the army, of whose ultimate loyalty General de Gaulle seemed in no doubt; they showed, too, that opinion in the country was behind him and that the majority of the Assembly was prepared to support him, though for different reasons, ranging from enthusiasm on the Left to impotent frustration on the part of some Gaullists and extreme right-wing Parliamentarians, who would have liked to oppose him if they had felt strong enough to do so.

One thing was abundantly clear. The end of the fighting would mark the beginning of a series of new, but no less difficult phases in Franco-Algerian relations. Would sufficient good-will be forthcoming on either side to create confidence among the Algerian electorate in the possibility of a free and fair vote? If Algeria chose association with France (the solution obviously hoped for by the General), would the right to opt for independence at some later date be open to her on, say, similar terms to those offered to member-States of the Community under article 86 of the Constitution? If this right were recognized, what would be the position of the Saharan regions, and what would be the likelihood of agreement regarding ownership and exploitation of Saharan oil? If different regions of Algeria voted differently, as was conceivable, could partition of Algeria be regarded as either practicable, or as offering any hopes of permanent peace?

In comparison with major problems such as these, the party skirmishing that took place regarding the constitutionality of the procedure outlined by General de Gaulle and other Government spokesmen seems trivial. Nevertheless, in view of all that has been said regarding the controversies and uncertainties surrounding Algeria's constitutional status, it is worth while noting that the offer appeared to some to raise constitutional difficulties. It was doubtful, for instance, whether Algeria's status could constitutionally be changed, except by a revision of the Constitution. There was some discussion on this point, but no obvious alternative was put forward.[1]

It may be, of course, that the procedure contemplated will be unchallengeable on constitutional grounds, even by the General's opponents. In any case, if General de Gaulle and the Government

[1] *v.* however M. Duverger's suggestion on this point in *Le Monde,* 19/8/59.

retain the confidence of the Assembly and the nation, the constitutionality of what he decides on and the Government agrees to, if ratified by Parliament and approved by the nation, cannot be challenged by any authority.

CHAPTER XI

De Gaulle's Republic

Attempts to analyse the working of the new institutions, comments on the evolution of the political situation and on the prospects of the Fifth Republic, all, almost without exception, come to one conclusion: the Fifth Republic could not have come into existence but for General de Gaulle and it is unlikely to continue to exist without him. The Fifth Republic is, by common consent, de Gaulle's Republic.

Is the Constitution irrelevant?

The Constitution itself is de Gaulle's constitution, though he himself would probably reject that view. Some concepts associated with Gaullism have no place in it—the functional second Chamber, for instance, and the corporatest elements that characterized some R.P.F. programmes.[1] Some of its most controversial articles (and possibly the most unworkable) owe more to politicians of the Fourth Republic than to General de Gaulle or his supporters. And M. Debré was responsible for the general conception and for the first working draft of the text of the Constitution.

Nevertheless, it is General de Gaulle's name that history will associate with the 1958 Constitution, and rightly so. As has already been pointed out, it bears the unmistakable imprints of some of his well-known ideas, in particular his concept of his own mission,

[1] The Government Bill on workers' participation in management, introduced during the first parliamentary session, is a reflection, though perhaps a pale one, of the principles of '*l'association capital-travail*'.

as expressed both in his formulation and in his interpretation of the three-fold rôle of the President. But the Fifth Republic is de Gaulle's Republic, in spite of, as well as because of the fact that its Constitution is largely his Constitution. Again and again in the preceding chapters doubts have been expressed regarding the possibility of this or that institution's being made to work if General de Gaulle were not there. Even his presence has not meant that they work as they were intended to. Moreover whatever he has achieved since he came to power owes little or nothing to the working of the Constitution, in so far as it has worked, and everything to his personality, in particular to his moral ascendancy. On the institutions themselves, critical comment has run the full gamut. One of the chief opponents of the régime, M. Mendès-France, (who is, like so many, a personal admirer of the General) described the institutions of the Fifth Republic as a façade hiding from the public the fact that 'for the time being, the destiny of the nation is in the hands of one man'.[1] Informed commentators who believe in the General, but not in his Constitution, have regarded them, either as a replica of the old—'the only real difference is the fundamental one that General de Gaulle is at the head of the State'[2]—or as constituting an archaic monstrosity. For Raymond Aron, 'The combination of an executive *à la* Louis XIV, and a Parliament disciplined *à l'anglaise* by the efforts of M. Debré is, in the long run, an impossibility.'[3]

The truth is that, except in the minds of General de Gaulle and of a few of his more impassioned and doctrinaire supporters, the Constitution is regarded by the politically-minded as either a temporary irritant, a minor or major lunacy, a Civil Servant's happy hunting ground, a technocratic paradise, a Parliamentarian's nightmare, a Republican face-saver, or a total irrelevancy. The non-politically minded do not think about it at all. A Radical Deputy, commenting on the 1946 Constitution at the time it was drawn up, said that, though the aim had been to produce something new and rational (*du neuf et du raisonnable*), the result was a Constitution in

[1] *Cahiers de la République*, June 1959.
[2] *Le Monde*, 13th May 1959.   [3] *Preuves*, June 1959.

which what was new was not rational and what was rational was not
new. When they voted in the referendum of 1958 the mass of the
French electorate were 'voting for something new, and handing
over the responsibility for being rational to General de Gaulle'.[1]
It was not a rational vote because they were voting not for a
Constitution, but for different political objectives and, where Algeria
was concerned, for a series of conflicting and incompatible miracles.
But in their minds, that part of the problem belonged henceforth
to General de Gaulle. The Fifth Republic is de Gaulle's Republic
because he, and he alone, was held to be able to work these miracles.

The Fifth Republic and Algeria

For the majority of public opinion, then, the Constitution is relevant in the immediate future only in so far as it can help to attain
these objectives, of which by far the most important is a solution of
the Algerian problem. The first test of the Fifth Republic's capacity to survive is General de Gaulle's ability to end the Algerian war,
or, failing that, his ability to retain the confidence of the nation
sufficiently to be allowed to go on trying to do so. If there is a loss
of faith in the present régime, similar to the loss of faith in the
Fourth Republic in 1958, then General de Gaulle and the Constitution might well disappear together and be replaced by some
form of dictatorship. Some of his opponents predict, and some of
his supporters fear, that General de Gaulle might become the unwilling instrument of an authoritarian régime. In either case, the
Fifth Republic as conceived by General de Gaulle would come to a
speedy end.

General de Gaulle himself has declared that he will never be the
representative of a faction.[2] Even among his opponents, he is
generally credited with 'a desire to be Washington, rather than
Louis Napoleon'.[3] It is notoriously hard for those who feel they
have a mission to abandon power, but General de Gaulle has done

---

[1] *Le Monde*, 8th January 1959.
[2] *v.* for instance, his press conference of 19th May 1958.
[3] André Philip in *Preuves*, February 1959, p. 4.

so once, and he has threatened to do so again. He has categoricall
denied that he would ever agree to exercise power except as th
representative of the nation.

The extent to which the danger of an army *coup* persists i
difficult to estimate, for, however much the French Army i
Algeria may have abandoned its traditional rôle of *la grand muett*
where politics are concerned, silence reigns on the matter of militar
opinion. Rumour, as well as a good deal of informed opinion, has i
that, in spite of the inconspicuous transfer of 1,500 officers to area
of activity less dangerous to the State than that of Algeria, the arm
still constituted a virtually autonomous force, at the end of th
first year of the new régime, and that General de Gaulle's failur
to commit himself to integration and to the maintenance o
French sovereignty in Algeria, and also to make it clear that h
would not contemplate negotiations with the rebels, had dis
appointed many of those who supported his return to power
Whether, if there were a renewed attempt at a *coup d'état*, it
authors could count on sufficient support if General de Gaulle wer
on the other side is a matter of considerable speculation.

In the country as a whole, the results of a year's effort seemed t
have left General de Gaulle's prestige as high as ever, though ther
were disappointments on some scores.

The balance sheet was impressive to some because a certain num
ber of things were done that Governments of the previous régim
had been unable to do. An agreement was reached with Tunisi
on the problem that had defeated the Government on the ev
of the crisis, the franc was devalued and an attempt made to pu
French finances in order, a beginning was made in the restora
tion of civilian authority in Algeria. It was disappointing to thos
whose hoped-for miracle did not happen and to those who felt tha
on the vital problem, the settlement of the political future of Algeria
the Fifth Republic seemed to be in much the same position as it
predecessor had been. The 1958 Assembly did, at least, have a clea
majority for a policy on Algeria, but it was a majority for a polic
of integration and the speeches made by the President of th

Republic revealed quite clearly that (as the Left had maintained all
along) he did not share these views. The first result was that, to the
deadlock created by France's inability to win the war or stop the
fighting, another was added, welcomed by the Left and resented by
the integrationists. General de Gaulle could not openly flout the
opinion of the Parliamentary majority. On the other hand, they
could not force him to make professions of faith in integration, or
to apply the policy, while his presence remained essential to them.
The U.N.R., in particular, had no *raison d'etre* other than its
Gaullism, which served a sadly divided party as an apology for a
policy.

Clearly, this stalemate over Algeria, though it could not last,
suited General de Gaulle very well, while he was playing for
time, hoping that it would help to reduce intransigence and bit-
terness on the Algerian problem and so make possible the creation
of a political atmosphere in which some solution might perhaps be
found.

The declaration of 16th September 1959 effectively ended the
period of apparent inactivity. Both its terms and its timing exploited
to the full whatever possibilities existed of mobilizing a majority of
French opinion for a firm and progressive policy. The sections of
opinion to which it proved most objectionable were precisely those
which had most appreciated the Government's achievements in the
fields of economic and foreign policy. The offer was couched in
terms that effectively called the bluff of extremists on both sides.
The Moslem nationalist movement had claimed that Moslems were
wholeheartedly in favour of independence; the settlers that they were
in favour of 'integration'. General de Gaulle's offer of *autodétermination* said, in effect, to both: 'Ask them, and see!' The majority
party in the Assembly, the U.N.R., was suffering from internal dis-
sensions and the unresolved controversies between its half-dozen or
so leaders increased the dependence of all of them on the one personality whose name could help to hold the movement together.
It dared not risk defeating the Government, since the price of so
doing was almost certain to be either the resignation of General de

N

Gaulle or a dissolution, and the movement was in no state to fac
the electorate as an opponent of the General, less than a year after i
had won an electoral victory on the strength of its fidelity to him
To army elements, anxious above all to prevent an F.L.N. victory
the declaration gave the assurance that there would be no politica
negotiations with the rebels and that a cease-fire would be followe
by a consultation of the whole Algerian population.

It was still far from certain, however, that peace in Algeria wa
just round the corner. General de Gaulle had staked his own future
along with that of the Fifth Republic, on a policy which, if i
succeeded, would constitute merely the first step along a road tha
on the most optimistic hypothesis, included a number of formidabl
obstacles to the speedy stabilization of Franco-Algerian relations
Nevertheless, the declaration was regarded by the majority o
opinion, both inside and outside France, as bringing peace neare
than it had been at any time since the outbreak of the rebellion i
1954.

The future of the Fifth Republic

But though peace in Algeria constituted the first test of the Fiftl
Republic's capacity to survive, it was by no means the only one
The second—and it was concurrent, not consecutive—was th
ability of the new régime to devise an efficient political machine
The first year saw a ferment of activity in a number of fields and th
introduction of a whole series of comprehensive reforms. Man'
Frenchmen had the feeling, for the first time for years, of being
both governed and administered. Yet the 'national renewal'
that General de Gaulle spoke of so frequently in his speeche
seemed limited to the fields of activity dealt with by the Hea
of the State and by the heads of Government departments. Parlia
ment and the public remained, for the most part, docile on
lookers. One political issue did arouse some interest—the questio
of State aid for Catholic schools. This does not point to any 're
newal' in political habits of thought. The Fifth Republic appeared
to many Frenchmen as well as to outsiders to be a paternalis

technocracy rather than a truly Parliamentary system, though whether it was an efficient technocracy was a matter on which grave doubts were expressed.

In this field, General de Gaulle's contribution may well be, in the long run, a hindrance rather than a help. He is not really interested in political machinery. He sees problems in terms of broad general principle and leaves the application to the relevant Ministers, who are regarded as technical executives—which is what most of them have been so far. The weakness of technocratic Governments, however, is that a series of departmental policies do not add up to a Government policy. A strong head of the State is not enough. Even if General de Gaulle's prestige enables him for the time being to count on continued docile support, and even that is doubtful when it comes to vital political decisions, he will not always be there. Sooner or later, it will be necessary for Governments to have coherent policies and that will mean the need for coherent majorities in Parliament.

The first Parliamentary sessions provided little evidence of any attempt by the political parties to look ahead or to think about the kind of political machine that the Fifth Republic ought to have. Some politicians are determined not to go back to 'the system' and the public is demonstrably out of sympathy with it. Yet if the political machine is not to be that of Parliamentary government as it existed under the Third and Fourth Republics, what is it to be? In the absence of any attempt to answer this question, there was a noticeable tendency for parties to revert to old quarrels, old slogans and familiar manoeuvres.[1]

One explanation for the passivity, or inactivity, of political leaders has been, no doubt, the dominating personality of General de Gaulle. His prestige among all sections of opinion in France

[1] The fact that the *Indépendents*, when exploring the possibilities of getting rid of M. Debré, were proposing to replace him by M. Bidault is indicative either of the strength of Fourth Republic habits, or of the poverty of Fifth Republic talent among right-wing members of the Assembly. The U.N.R. has only M. Soustelle who is of Prime Ministerial calibre and he has not yet established himself as leader of the party.

(except for the Communists), in Algeria (particularly among the Moslem population) and in Africa, has made him essential and un-opposable, and the gap between the quality of his leadership and that of the political parties has made the emergence of any successor seem impossible while he is there.

But the problem goes deeper than that. General de Gaulle's conception of national leadership is one that helps to inhibit the development of political machinery, that encourages the tendency to hand over responsibility to him. He believes in the existence of a fundamental national unity, underlying political divisions, in a kind of Rousseauistic 'general will'. He thinks that

> This essential unity, independent of beliefs and passions, can be discovered objectively by everyone, provided only that they have non-partisan and reasonably competent minds.[1]

His mission is to be the incarnation of this unity, which can restore France's moral and political greatness and allow her to exercise in the world the influence that belongs to her by virtue of centuries of history.

In moments of great crisis, such as the French defeat of 1940, a leader who can, thus, incarnate the national spirit can save the self-respect and even the life of a nation, as General de Gaulle helped to do between 1940 and 1944. It is far from certain that leadership of this kind can be equally powerful in peace-time, and particularly in a crisis such as that of May 1958, whose gravest symptom was precisely the failure of the general public to recognize it as a crisis that called for any positive or prolonged effort on their part. The crisis of war, in itself, helps to unite, because it is an overwhelming, and essentially simple challenge to national existence that calls for the immediate mobilization of every resource. The crises of peace, political, economic, or even constitutional, are never easy to under-stand. They can be insidious, long-lasting and divisive and their cure demands effective political machinery as well as leadership.

[1] André Philip in *Preuves*, November 1958, p. 19.

General de Gaulle is not merely uninterested in political machinery; he is profoundly out of harmony with both the theory and the practice of twentieth-century Parliamentary government. He is a uniter, and Parliamentary government is essentially the organization of divergencies, with a view to reducing them to coherent alternative policies. Parliament is based on the assumption that differences within a nation are profound and permanent and that there may be no underlying unity. The gulf between General de Gaulle's mind and that of the French Parliament is wide and, at times, unbridgeable.

The danger to the future of the Fifth Republic of a combination of government by technicians and Parliamentary inefficacity is twofold. It is, first, that Cabinet government, which was weak and divided under the Fourth Republic, may become anarchic under the Fifth; and second that political leaders, divided into those who reject the 'system' of the Third and Fourth Republics, and those who, privately, would like to go back to it, may prove incapable of either going back or looking forward. The danger is not immediate, perhaps, while the problem that brought about the explosion of 1958 is still there, and renders General de Gaulle's leadership essential. But the basic weaknesses of the French Parliamentary system, which underlay the crisis, are still there too. The only real difference is the presence of General de Gaulle. The Fifth Republic will not be secure until de Gaulle's Republic has become the French Republic.

The French Constitution of October 4th, 1958[1]

PREAMBLE

The French people solemnly proclaim their attachment to the Rights of man and to the principles of national sovereignty as defined by the Declaration of 1789, confirmed and completed by the Preamble to the Constitution of 1946.

By virtue of these principles and of that of the free determination of peoples, the Republic offers to those Overseas territories which express a desire to accept membership of them new institutions founded on the common ideal of liberty, equality and fraternity and conceived with a view to their democratic evolution.

Article 1. The Republic and those peoples of the Overseas territories who, by an act of free determination, adopt the present Constitution set up a Community.

The Community is founded upon the equality and solidarity of the peoples composing it.

TITLE I

SOVEREIGNTY

Article 2. France is an indivisible, secular, democratic and social Republic. It ensures the equality before the law of all citizens, without distinction of origin, race or religion. It respects all beliefs.

The national emblem is the tricolour flag, blue, white and red.

The national anthem is the '*Marseillaise*'.

[1] This translation is by William Pickles and is taken from his *French Constitution of October 4th, 1958* (Stevens, London, 1960).

The motto of the Republic is 'Liberty, Equality, Fraternity'.

Its principle is government of the people, by the people, for the people.

Article 3. National sovereignty belongs to the people, who exercise it through their representatives and by way of referendum.

No section of the people and no individual may claim to exercise it.

The suffrage may be direct or indirect in conditions provided for by the Constitution. It is in all cases universal, equal and secret. The right to vote, in conditions laid down by law, is enjoyed by all French nationals of either sex who are of age and in full possession of their civil and political rights.

Article 4. Parties and political groups play a part in the exercise of the right to vote. The right to form parties and their freedom of action are unrestricted. They must respect the principles of national sovereignty and of democracy.

TITLE II

THE PRESIDENT OF THE REPUBLIC

Article 5. The President of the Republic endeavours to ensure respect for the Constitution. He provides, by his arbitration, for the regular functioning of the public authorities and the continuity of the State.

He is the protector of the independence of the nation, of the integrity of its territory, of respect for treaties and Community agreements.

Article 6. The President of the Republic is elected for seven years by an electoral college which includes the members of Parliament, of the Departmental Councils, and of the Assemblies of Overseas territories, in addition to the elected representatives of the Municipal Councils.

These representatives are:

the Mayor for *communes* of less than 1,000 inhabitants;

the Mayor and first Deputy-Mayor for *communes* of 1,000 to 2,000 inhabitants;

the Mayor, first Deputy-Mayor and the municipal Councillor having received the highest vote in the municipal elections, for *communes* of 2,001 to 2,500 inhabitants;

the Mayor and first two Deputy-Mayors for *communes* of 2,501 to 3,000 inhabitants;

the Mayor, the first two Deputy-Mayors and the three municipal

Councillors having received the highest votes, for *communes* of 3,001 to 6,000 inhabitants;

the Mayor, the first two Deputy-Mayors and the six Councillors having received the highest votes, for *communes* of 6,001 to 9,000 inhabitants;

all the municipal Councillors for *communes* of more than 9,000 inhabitants;

in addition, for *communes* of more than 30,000 inhabitants, delegates nominated by the Municipal Council at the rate of one for every thousand inhabitants after the first 30,000.

In the Overseas territories of the Republic, the electoral college also includes representatives elected by the Councils of the administrative entities, in the conditions laid down in an organic law.

The representation of member States of the Community in the college electing the President of the Republic is determined by agreement between the Republic and the member States of the Community.

The methods of application of the present article are determined by an organic law.

Article 7. The President is elected at the first ballot, if an absolute majority is obtained. If this is not obtained at the first ballot, the President of the Republic is elected at the second ballot by a relative majority.

Voting begins at the time fixed by the Government.

The election of the new President takes place not less than twenty and not more than fifty days before the expiry of the existing President's term of office.

If, for whatever reason, the Presidency of the Republic falls vacant, or if the incapacity of the President has been certified by the Constitutional Council, at the request of the Government and by an absolute majority of its members, the functions of the President, except those conferred by articles 11 and 12 below, are performed temporarily by the President of the Senate. When a vacancy occurs, or when the incapacity is certified by the Constitutional Council to be permanent, and unless *force majeure* has been certified by the Constitutional Council, the election of a new President takes place not less than twenty and not more than fifty days after the opening of the vacancy or the declaration of the permanence of the incapacity.

Article 8. The President of the Republic appoints the Prime Minister. He terminates his period of office on the presentation by the Prime Minister of the resignation of the Government.

He appoints and dismisses the other members of the Government on the proposal of the Prime Minister.

Article 9. The President of the Republic presides over the Council of Ministers.

Article 10. The President of the Republic promulgates laws within the fortnight following their final adoption and transmission to the Government.

Before the end of this period, he may ask Parliament to reconsider the whole law or specified articles. This reconsideration cannot be refused.

Article 11. On the proposal of the Government during Parliamentary sessions, or on the joint proposal of the two Assemblies, published in the *Journal Officiel*, the President of the Republic may submit to a referendum any Government Bill dealing with the organisation of the public authorities, approving a Community agreement or authorizing the ratification of a treaty which, although not in conflict with the Constitution, would affect the working of institutions.

If the result of the referendum is favourable to the adoption of the Bill, the President of the Republic promulgates it within the time-limit laid down in the preceding article.

Article 12. The President of the Republic may pronounce the dissolution of the National Assembly, after consulting the Prime Minister and the Presidents of the Assemblies.

A general election takes place not less than twenty and not more than forty days after the dissolution.

The National Assembly meets as of right on the second Thursday following its election. If this meeting takes place outside the periods fixed for ordinary sessions, a session opens as of right for a period of a fortnight.

No new dissolution may take place during the year following these elections.

Article 13. The President of the Republic signs such ordinances and decrees as have been considered by the Council of Ministers. He appoints to the civil and military posts of the State. Councillors of State, the Grand Chancellor of the Legion of Honour, Ambassadors and Envoys Extraordinary, Senior Councillors of the Court of Accounts, Prefects, Government representatives in Overseas Territories, General Officers, Flag

Officers, Air-Marshals, Rectors of Academies and *directeurs* of Government departments are appointed in the Council of Ministers. An organic law determines the other appointments to be made in the Council of Ministers, as also the conditions in which the appointing power of the President of the Republic may be delegated by him and be exercised in his name.

Article 14. The President of the Republic accredits Ambassadors and Envoys Extraordinary to foreign powers; foreign Ambassadors and Envoys Extraordinary are accredited to him.

Article 15. The President of the Republic is Head of the armed forces. He presides over the Higher Councils and Committees of National Defence.

Article 16. When there exists a serious and immediate threat to the institutions of the Republic, the independence of the Nation, the integrity of its territory or the fulfilment of its international obligations, and the regular functioning of the constitutional public authorities has been interrupted, the President of the Republic takes the measures required by the circumstances, after consulting officially the Prime Minister, the Presidents of the Assemblies and the Constitutional Council.

He informs the Nation of these matters by a message.

These measures must be inspired by the desire to ensure to the constitutional public authorities, with the minimum of delay, the means of fulfilling their functions. The Constitutional Council is consulted about them.

Parliaments meet as of right.

The National Assembly cannot be dissolved during the [period of] exercise of the exceptional powers.

Article 17. The President of the Republic has the right of pardon.

Article 18. The President of the Republic communicates with the two Assemblies of Parliament by means of messages which are read for him and on which there is no debate.

If Parliament is not in session, it is specially summoned for this purpose.

Article 19. The acts of the President of the Republic other than those provided for in articles 8 (para. 1), 11, 12, 16, 18, 54, 56 and 61 are countersigned by the Prime Minister and, where necessary, by the appropriate Ministers.

TITLE III

THE GOVERNMENT

Article 20. The Government decides and directs the policy of the nation. It has at its disposal the administration and the armed forces.

It is responsible to Parliament in the conditions and in accordance with the procedures laid down in Articles 49 and 50.

Article 21. The Prime Minister is in general charge of the work of the Government. He is responsible for National Defence. He ensures the execution of laws. Except as provided for under Article 13, he exercises rule-making power and appoints to civil and military posts.

He may delegate certain of his powers to the Ministers.

He deputises for the President of the Republic, when necessary, as Chairman of the Councils and Committees referred to in Article 15.

In exceptional circumstances, he may deputise for him as Chairman of the Council of Ministers, by virtue of an explicit delegation of authority and with a specific agenda.

Article 22. The acts of the Prime Minister are countersigned, where necessary, by the Ministers responsible for their execution.

Article 23. Membership of the Government is incompatible with that of Parliament, with the representation of any trade or professional organization on the national level, with any public employment or professional activity.

An organic law lays down the conditions in which the holders of the above offices, functions or employments are to be replaced.

Members of Parliament are replaced in the manner laid down in Article 25.

TITLE IV

PARLIAMENT

Article 24. Parliament is composed of the National Assembly and the Senate. The Deputies of the National Assembly are elected by direct, universal suffrage.

The Senate is elected by indirect suffrage. It represents the territorial entities of the Republic. French citizens resident abroad are represented in the Senate.

Article 25. An organic law determines the length of life of each assembly, the number of its members, the payment made to them, the rules concerning qualification for and disqualification from election and the incompatibility of certain functions with membership of Parliament.

This organic law also determines the manner of election of those who, in the event of a vacancy, replace Deputies and Senators until the next election, general or partial, to the assembly in which the vacancy occurs.

Article 26. No member of Parliament may be prosecuted, sought out, arrested, held in custody or tried on account of opinions expressed or votes cast by him in the exercise of his functions.

No member of Parliament may be prosecuted or arrested on account of any crime or misdemeanour during a parliamentary session, without the consent of the Assembly of which he is a member, except when the member is arrested *flagrante delicto*.

Members of Parliament may be arrested when Parliament is not in session only with the authorization of the *bureau* of the Assembly of which they are members, except when the arrest is *flagrante delicto*, when the prosecution has [already] been authorized or the final sentence pronounced.

Members are released from custody or their prosecution is suspended if the Assembly of which they are members so demands.

Article 27. Any specific instruction to a member of Parliament [from an outside body] is null and void.

The member's right to vote belongs to him alone.

The (*sic*) organic law may authorize the delegation of the right to vote in exceptional circumstances. In these cases, no member may cast more than one delegated vote.

Article 28. Parliament meets as of right in two ordinary sessions per year.

The first session begins on the first Tuesday of October and ends on the third Friday of December.

The second session begins on the last Tuesday of April; it may not last more than three months.

Article 29. At the request of the Prime Minister or of the majority of the members of the National Assembly, Parliament meets in special session, with a specified agenda.

When the special session is held at the request of members of the National Assembly, the closure decree is read as soon as Parliament has completed the agenda for which it was called and at most twelve days after its meeting.

Only the Prime Minister can ask for a new session before the end of the month following the date of the closure decree.

Article 30. Except when Parliament meets as of right, special sessions are opened and closed by decree of the President of the Republic.

Article 31. Members of the Government have access to both Assemblies. They are heard when they so request.

They may be assisted by Government commissioners.

Article 32. The President of the National Assembly is elected for the life of each Parliament. The President of the Senate is elected after each partial renewal.

Article 33. The sittings of both Assemblies are public. A full report of debates is published in the *Journal Officiel.*

Each assembly may meet in secret session at the request of the Prime Minister or of one-tenth of its members.

TITLE V

RELATIONS BETWEEN PARLIAMENT AND GOVERNMENT
Article 34. Laws are voted by Parliament.

Laws determine the rules concerning:

civic rights and the fundamental guarantees of the public liberties of the citizen; the obligations of citizens, as regards their persons and property, for purposes of National Defence;

the nationality, status and legal capacity of persons, property in marriage, inheritance and gifts;

the definitions of crimes and misdemeanours and of the penalties applicable to them; criminal procedure, amnesty, the creation of new orders of jurisdiction and the statute of the judiciary;

the basis of assessment, rate and methods of collection of taxes of all kinds; the currency system.

Laws determine also the rules concerning:

the electoral system for Parliamentary and local assemblies;

the creation of categories of public corporation;

the fundamental guarantees of civil servants and members of the armed forces;

nationalizations and the transfer of property from the public to the private sectors.

Laws determine the fundamental principles;

of the general organization of National Defence;
of the free administration of local entities, of their powers and of their resources;
of education;
of the law of property, of real-property rights and of civil and commercial contract;
of labour law, trade-union law and social security.

Finance laws determine the resources and obligations of the State, in the manner and with the reservations provided for in an organic law.

Programme-laws determine the purposes of the social and economic action of the State.

The provisions of the present article may be completed and more closely defined by an organic law.

Article 35. Declarations of war are authorized by Parliament.

Article 36. A state of siege is decreed in the Council of Ministers. Its prolongation beyond twelve days can be authorized only by Parliament

Article 37. Matters other than those regulated by laws fall within the field of rule-making.

Documents in the form of laws, but dealing with matters falling within the rule-making field may be modified by decree issued after consultation with the Council of State. Such of these documents as come into existence after the coming into force of the present Constitution may be modified by decree only if the Constitutional Council has declared them to be within the rule-making sphere, by virtue of the previous paragraph.

Article 38. With a view to carrying out its programme, the Government may seek the authorization of Parliament, for a limited period of time, to issue ordinances regulating matters normally falling within the field of law-making.

(The) ordinances are made in the Council of Ministers after consultation with the Council of State. They come into force upon publication, but cease to be effective if the Bill ratifying them is not laid before Parliament by the date fixed by the enabling Act.

At the expiration of the period mentioned in paragraph 1 of this

Article, (the) ordinances may be modified only by law, as regards matters falling within the field of law.

Article 39. Legislative initiative is exercised by the Prime Minister and by members of Parliament.

Government Bills are considered in the Council of Ministers, after consultation with the Council of State and laid before one of the two assemblies. Finance Bills are submitted first to the National Assembly.

Article 40. Private members' Bills, resolutions and amendments which, if passed, would reduce public revenues or create or increase charges on the revenue are out of order.

Article 41. If, in the course of legislative procedure, it becomes apparent that a private members' proposal or amendment does not fall within the field of law-making, or is in conflict with powers delegated by virtue of Article 38, the Government may demand that it be declared out of order.

In the event of disagreement between the Government and the President of the Assembly concerned, the Constitutional Council gives a ruling, at the request of either party, within a week.

Article 42. Government Bills are discussed, in the assembly to which they are first submitted, on the basis of the Government's text.

An assembly debating a Bill transmitted from the other assembly discusses it on the basis of the text transmitted to it.

Article 43. Government and private members' Bills are sent, at the request of the Government, or of the assembly then discussing them, to Commissions specially appointed for this purpose.

Bills of either type for which such a request has not been made are sent to one of the permanent Commissions, the number of which is limited to six for each assembly.

Article 44. Members of Parliament and the Government have the right of amendment.

When the debate has begun, the Government may object to the discussion of any amendment which has not previously been submitted to the Commission.

If the Government so requests, the assembly concerned accepts or rejects by a single vote the whole or part of the Bill or motion under discussion, together with such amendments as have been proposed or accepted by the Government.

Article 45. Every Government or private member's Bill is discussed successively in the two assemblies with a view to agreement on identical versions.

When, as a result of disagreement between the two assemblies, a Bill has not been passed after two readings in each assembly, or, if the Government has declared the Bill urgent, after a single reading by each assembly, the Prime Minister is entitled to have the Bill sent to a joint Committee composed of equal numbers from the two assemblies, with the task of finding agreed versions of the provisions in dispute.

The version prepared by the joint committee may be submitted by the Government to the two assemblies for their approval. No amendment may be accepted without the agreement of the Government.

If the joint committee does not produce an agreed version, or if the version agreed is not approved as provided for in the preceding paragraph, the Government may ask the National Assembly, after one more reading by the National Assembly and by the Senate, to decide the matter. In this case, the National Assembly may adopt either the version prepared by the joint committee or the last version passed by itself, modified, if necessary, by one or any of the amendments passed by the Senate.

Article 46. Laws to which the Constitution gives the status of organic laws are passed or amended in the following conditions.

The Bill, whether Government or private member's, is not debated or voted on in the first assembly in which it is introduced until a fortnight after its introduction.

The procedure of Article 45 applies. Nevertheless, if the two assemblies fail to agree, the Bill may become law only if it is passed at its final reading in the National Assembly by an absolute majority of its members.

Organic laws relating to the Senate must be passed in the same terms by both assemblies.

Organic laws may be promulgated only when the Constitutional Council has certified their conformity with the Constitution.

Article 47. An organic law lays down the conditions in which Parliament votes Finance Bills.

If the National Assembly has not concluded its first reading within forty days from the introduction of the Bill, the Government sends the Bill to the Senate, which must reach a decision within a fortnight. Subsequent procedure is that provided for in Article 45.

If Parliament has reached no decision within seventy days, the provisions of the Bill may be put into force by ordinance.

If the Finance Bill determining revenue and expenditure for the financial year has not been introduced in time to be promulgated before the beginning of the financial year, the Government asks Parliament, as a matter of urgency, for authorization to levy the taxes voted and to allocate by decree the sums necessary for estimates already approved.

The time limits fixed by the present article are suspended when Parliament is not in session.

The Court of Accounts assists Parliament and the Government to supervise the application of Finance Acts.

Article 48. The agenda of the assemblies gives priority, in the order determined by the Government, to the discussion of Government Bills and private members' Bills accepted by the Government.

Priority is given at one sitting per week to the questions of members of Parliament and the replies of the Government.

Article 49. The Prime Minister, after deliberation in the Council of Ministers, pledges the responsibility of the Government before the National Assembly, on its programme or, if it be so decided, on a general declaration of policy.

The National Assembly challenges the responsibility of the Government by passing a vote of censure. A censure motion is in order only if it is signed by at least one-tenth of the members of the National Assembly. The vote may not take place until forty-eight hours after its introduction. Only votes in favour of the censure motion are counted, and the motion is carried only if it receives the votes of the majority of the members of the Assembly. If the censure motion is rejected, its signatories may not propose a further one during the same session, except in the case provided for in the next paragraph.

The Prime Minister may, after deliberation in the Council of Ministers, pledge the responsibility of the Government before the National Assembly on the passing of all or part of a Bill or a motion. In this case, the Bill or part of Bill or motion is regarded as having been passed, unless a censure motion, put down within the following twenty-four hours, is passed in the conditions provided for in the previous paragraph.

The Prime Minister is entitled to seek the approval of the Senate for a general statement of policy.

o

Article 50. When the National Assembly passes a motion of censure or rejects the Government's programme or a general statement of Government policy, the Prime Minister must tender to the President of the Republic the resignation of the Government.

Article 51. The closure of ordinary or special sessions is automatically postponed, if need be, in order to permit the application of the provisions of Article 49.

TITLE VI

TREATIES AND INTERNATIONAL AGREEMENTS

Article 52. The President of the Republic negotiates and ratifies treaties.

He is informed of the negotiation of any international agreement not subject to ratification.

Article 53. Peace treaties, commercial treaties, treaties or agreements concerning international organization, those which involve the State in financial obligations, modify the provisions of the law, concern personal status or involve the cession, exchange or addition of territory may be ratified or approved only by virtue of a law.

They take effect only after having been ratified or approved.

No cession, exchange or addition of territory is valid without the consent of the populations concerned.

Article 54. If the Constitutional Council, consulted by the President of the Republic, the Prime Minister or the President of either assembly, has declared that an international obligation includes a clause contrary to the Constitution, authorization to ratify or approve it may be accorded only after revision of the Constitution.

Article 55. Treaties or agreements regularly ratified or approved have, from the time of publication, an authority superior to that of laws, provided, in the case of each agreement or treaty, that it is applied by the other party.

TITLE VII

THE CONSTITUTIONAL COUNCIL

Article 56. The Constitutional Council has nine members, whose term of office lasts for nine years and is not renewable. Its members are appointed by thirds every three years. Three members are nominated by the President of the Republic, three by the President of the National Assembly, three by the President of the Senate.

In addition to the nine members provided for above, former Presidents of the Republic are *ex officio* life-members of the Constitutional Council.

The President is appointed by the President of the Republic. He has a casting vote.

Article 57. The functions of a member of the Constitutional Council are incompatible with those of a Minister or member of Parliament.

Other positions incompatible with membership of the Council are listed in an organic law.

Article 58. The Constitutional Council supervises the election of the President of the Republic, with a view to ensuring its regularity.

It investigates objections and proclaims the result.

Article 59. The Constitutional Council decides, in disputed cases, on the regularity of the election of Deputies and Senators.

Article 60. The Constitutional Council supervises the conduct of referenda with a view to ensuring their regularity, and proclaims the results.

Article 61. Organic laws, before their promulgation, and the rules of procedure of the Parliamentary assemblies, before their application, must be submitted to the Constitutional Council, which pronounces on their conformity with the Constitution.

For the same purpose, [ordinary] laws may be submitted to the Constitutional Council, before their promulgation, by the President of the Republic, the Prime Minister or the President of either assembly.

In the cases provided for in the two preceding paragraphs, the Constitutional Council decides within a month. At the request of the Government, however, if the matter is urgent, this period may be reduced to a week.

In these above-mentioned cases, reference to the Constitutional Council prolongs the period allowed for promulgation.

Article 62. A provision declared unconstitutional may not be promulgated or applied.

Decisions of the Constitutional Council are not subject to appeal. They are binding on public authorities and on all administrative and judicial authorities.

Article 63. An organic law lays down the organization and methods of working of the Constitutional Council, the procedures to be followed in referring matters to it and in particular the time-limits within which disputes may be laid before it.

TITLE VIII

THE JUDICIAL AUTHORITY

Article 64. The President of the Republic is the protector of the independence of the judicial authority.

He is assisted by the Higher Council of the Judiciary.

An organic law regulates the position of the Judiciary. Judges are irremovable.

Article 65. The Higher Council of the Judiciary is presided over by the President of the Republic. The Minister of Justice is *ex officio* its Vice-President. He may deputise for the President of the Republic.

The Higher Council has in addition nine members appointed by the President of the Republic in the conditions laid down by an organic law.

The Higher Council of the Judiciary submits nominations for appointments to the supreme Court of Appeal (*Cour de Cassation*) and to the posts of First President of Assize Courts (*Cours d'Appel*). It gives its opinion, in conditions laid down by the organic law, on the proposals of the Minister of Justice concerning the appointment of other Judges. It is consulted on reprieves in conditions laid down by an organic law.

The Higher Council of the Judiciary sits as the Disciplinary Council for Judges. It is then presided over by the First President of the *Cour de Cassation*.

Article 66. None may be arbitrarily detained.

The judicial authority, guardian of the liberty of the individual, ensures respect for this principle in conditions determined by the law.

TITLE IX

THE HIGH COURT OF JUSTICE

Article 67. A High Court of Justice is instituted.

It is composed of members elected, from their own numbers and in equal parts, by the National Assembly and the Senate, after each election to these assemblies. It elects its President from among its members.

An organic law determines the composition of the High Court, its rules of operation and the procedure applicable before it.

Article 68. The President of the Republic is responsible for actions performed in the carrying out of his duties only in case of high treason. He can be indicted only by identical motions passed by the two assemblies by open ballot and by an absolute majority of their members; he is tried by the High Court of Justice.

Members of the Government are penally responsible for actions performed in the carrying out of their duties and classed as crimes or misdemeanours at the time when they were committed. The procedure set out above is applicable to them and to their accomplices in cases of plotting against the security of the State. In the cases provided for in this paragraph, the High Court is bound by the definitions of the crimes and misdemeanours and by the rules as to penalties to be found in the criminal laws in force at the times when the actions were performed.

TITLE X

THE ECONOMIC AND SOCIAL COUNCIL

Article 69. The Economic and Social Council gives its opinion, at the request of the Government, on such Government Bills, draft ordinances, draft decrees and private members' Bills as are submitted to it.

A member of the Economic and Social Council may be appointed by the Council to appear before the parliamentary assemblies and put forward the opinion of the Council on Bills submitted to it.

Article 70. The Economic and Social Council may also be consulted by the Government on any economic or social problem concerning the Republic or the Community. Any plan or programme-Bill of economic or social character is submitted to it for its opinion.

Article 71. The composition of the Economic and Social Council and its methods of work are laid down in an organic law.

TITLE XI

TERRITORIAL ENTITIES

Article 72. The territorial entities of the Republic are the *communes*, the *départements* and the Overseas Territories. Any other territorial entity is created by law.

These entities are freely administered by elected councils in conditions laid down by law.

In the *départements* and territories, the Government delegate is responsible for the interests of the nation, supervises the administration and ensures the observance of the law.

Article 73. The status as defined by law and the administrative organization of the Overseas *départements* may be modified by measures intended to adapt them to local conditions.

Article 74. The Overseas Territories of the Republic have a special organization which takes account of the interests of each within the framework of the general interests of the Republic. This organization is laid down and modified by law, after consultation with the Territorial Assembly of the Territory concerned.

Article 75. Citizens of the Republic who do not enjoy ordinary civil status, the only status to which Article 34 may be construed as referring, keep their personal status so long as they have not renounced it.

Article 76. Overseas Territories may keep their status within the Republic. If they express the desire to do so, by a decision of their Territorial Assembly, within the period fixed by Article 91, para. 1, they become either Overseas *départements* or, grouped together or separately, member States of the Community.

TITLE XII

THE COMMUNITY

Article 77. In the Community established by the present Constitution, the States enjoy autonomy; they administer themselves and manage their own affairs, freely and democratically.

There is in the Community only one citizenship.

All citizens are equal before the law, whatever their origin, race or religion. They have the same duties.

Article 78. The field of competence of the Community includes foreign policy, defence, currency, common economic and financial policy and policy concerning strategic raw materials.

It also includes, in the absence of a special agreement to the contrary, supervision of justice, higher education, the general organization of external and common transport, and telecommunications.

Special agreements may establish other common fields of competence or provide for any transfer of competence from the Community to one of its members.

Article 79. The member States come within the provisions of Article 77 as soon as they have made the choice provided for in Article 76.

Until the coming into force of the measures necessary for the application of the present Title, matters of common competence will be dealt with by the Republic.

Article 80. The President of the Republic presides over and represents the Community.

The latter has as its organs an Executive Council, a Senate and a Court of Arbitration.

Article 81. The member States of the Community take part in the election of the President in the conditions provided for in Article 6.

The President of the Republic, in his capacity of President of the Community, is represented in each State of the Community.

Article 82. The Executive Council of the Community is presided over by the President of the Community. It is composed of the Prime Minister of the Republic, the Heads of Government of each of the member States, and the Ministers made responsible, on behalf of the Community, for common affairs.

The Executive Council organises governmental and administrative co-operation between the members of the Community.

The organisation and methods of work of the Executive Council are determined by an organic law.

Article 83. The Senate of the Community is composed of delegates chosen from among their own number by the Parliament of the Republic and the legislative assemblies of the other members. The number of delegates from each State is fixed in a manner which takes account of its population and of the responsibilities which it assumes within the Community.

It holds two sessions a year, which are opened and closed by the President of the Community and may not last longer than one month each.

At the request of the President, it discusses common economic and financial policy before the Parliament of the Republic and, in appropriate circumstances, the legislative assemblies of other members of the Community pass laws in this field.

The Senate of the Community considers the acts, international agreements, and treaties referred to in Articles 35 and 53, where these involve obligations for the Community.

It takes binding decisions in the fields in which power has been delegated to it by the legislative assemblies of members of the Community. The decisions are promulgated in the States concerned in the same ways as the laws of the territories.

An organic law determines its composition and the rules under which it functions.

Article 84. A Court of Arbitration of the Community gives rulings on disputes between members of the Community.

Its composition and powers are determined by an organic law.

Article 85. Notwithstanding the procedure provided for in Article 89, the provisions of the present Title concerning the functioning of the common institutions of the Community are revised by laws couched in the same terms passed by the Parliament of the Republic and by the Senate of the Community.

Article 86. A change of the status of a member State of the Community may be requested either by the Republic, or by a resolution of the legislative assembly of the State concerned, confirmed by a local referendum, organized and supervised by the institutions of the Community. The methods by which the change of status is made are determined by an agreement approved by the Parliament of the Republic and the legislative assembly concerned.

In the same manner, a member State of the Community may become independent. It thereby ceases to belong to the Community.

Article 87. Special agreements concluded in application of the present title require the approval of the Parliament of the Republic and of the legislative assembly concerned.

TITLE XIII

AGREEMENTS OF ASSOCIATION

Article 88. The Republic or the Community may conclude agreements with States desiring to form an association with either, in order to develop their civilizations.

TITLE XIV

REVISION

Article 89. The right to propose amendments to the Constitution belongs concurrently to the President of the Republic, on the proposal of the Prime Minister, and to members of Parliament.

The amending project or proposal must be passed by the two assemblies in the identical terms. The amendment becomes effective when it has been approved by referendum.

However, the amending project is not submitted to a referendum when the President of the Republic decides to submit it to Parliament, meeting as Congress; in this case the amendment is accepted only if it obtains a majority of three-fifths of the votes cast. The Bureau of the Congress is that of the National Assembly.

The amendment procedure may not be initiated or pursued when the integrity of the territory is under attack.

The Republican form of government is not subject to revision.

TITLE XV

TEMPORARY DISPOSITIONS

Article 90. The ordinary session of Parliament is suspended. The term of office of the members of the present National Assembly will expire on the day the Assembly elected by virtue of the present Constitution meets.

Until this meeting, only the Government has authority to summon Parliament.

The term of office of the members of the Assembly of the French Union will expire at the same time as the term of the members of the present National Assembly.

Article 91. The institutions of the Republic provided for in the present Constitution will be set up within a period of four months from the day of its promulgation.

This period is extended to six months for the institutions of the Community.

The powers of the present President of the Republic will expire only on the proclamation of the results of the election provided for in Articles 6 and 7 of the present Constitution.

The member States of the Community will take part in this first election in conditions appropriate to their status at the date of the promulgation of the Constitution.

The established authorities will continue to exercise their functions in these States in accordance with the laws and other instruments applicable on the date at which the Constitution enters into force, until the installation of the authorities provided for by their new form of government.

Until its constitution has been finally determined, the Senate consists of the present members of the Council of the Republic. The organic laws which will determine the final constitution of the Senate must come into existence before July 31, 1959.

The powers conferred on the Constitutional Council by Articles 58 and 59 of the Constitution will be exercised, until the installation of the Council, by a Commission composed of the Vice-President of the Council of State as chairman, the First President of the *Cour de Cassation* and the First President of the Court of Accounts.

The peoples of the member States of the Community continue to be represented in Parliament until the coming into force of the measures necessary for the application of Title XII.

Article 92. The legislative measures necessary for the installation of the institutions and, until that installation, for the functioning of the public authorities, will be taken in the Council of Ministers, after consultation with the Council of State, by ordinances having the force of law.

During the period prescribed in the first paragraph of Article 91 the Government is authorized to determine, by ordinances having the force of law and issued in the same form, the electoral system for the assemblies provided for by the Constitution.

During the same period and in the same conditions, the Government may also take, on any subject, such measures as it may consider necessary to the life of the nation, the protection of the citizens or the preservation of freedom.

The present law will be applied as the Constitution of the Republic and of the Community.

Index